First Time Home Buyers Guide

Everything You Need To Know Before Buying Your First House

By

Ernie Braveboy

Your Free Gift

Before you read another word, I have a wonderful gift, just for you. Download the free eBook, "Real Estate Marketing: How to be A Real-Estate Millionaire," to learn secrets that have made me millions in my career in real estate.

https://ebraveboy_3ee2.gr8.com/

© **Copyright 2020 by Ernie Braveboy - All rights reserved.**

This document is geared towards providing exact and reliable information in regards to the topic and issue covered. The publication is sold with the idea that the publisher is not required to render accounting, officially permitted or otherwise qualified services. If advice is necessary, legal or professional, a practiced individual in the profession should be ordered.

- From a Declaration of Principles which was accepted and approved equally by a Committee of the American Bar Association and a Committee of Publishers and Associations.

In no way is it legal to reproduce, duplicate, or transmit any part of this document in either electronic means or printed format. Recording of this publication is strictly prohibited, and any storage of this document is not allowed unless with written permission from the publisher. All rights reserved.

The information provided herein is stated to be truthful and consistent, in that any liability, in terms of inattention or otherwise, by any usage or abuse of any policies, processes, or directions contained within is the solitary and utter responsibility of the recipient reader. Under no circumstances will any legal responsibility or blame be held against the publisher for any reparation, damages, or monetary loss due to the information herein, either directly or indirectly.

Respective authors own all copyrights not held by the publisher.

The information herein is offered for informational purposes solely and is universal as so. The presentation of the information is without a contract or any type of guarantee assurance.

The trademarks that are used are without any consent, and the publication of the trademark is without permission or backing by the trademark owner. All trademarks and brands within this book are for clarifying purposes only and are owned by the owners themselves, not affiliated with this document.

Introduction

Congratulations and welcome to ***"First time home buyers guide: everything you need to know before buying your first house."***

So you've worked hard all these years and have come to the point where you feel owning a home is something you want to accomplish. Or maybe you are still on your way and can see yourself owning a home in a few months or years to come. Kudos to you.

But...

For some reason, you feel totally clueless about the impending financial decision ahead because you don't know a thing about real estate. After all, you've never bought a house before in your life. You don't know what potential mistakes you could make. You don't know what to do to keep from getting screwed on a deal.

If you have these and many other concerns, then you have sharp instincts. And you have every right to reason along such lines. This is because, like many areas in life, when buying a home, what you don't know can hurt or even kill you.

You see, buying a home will potentially be the biggest financial decision you will ever make in your life. In fact, it can actually be described as a life event. It is a very large financial and personal commitment that can make a very big difference to your bottom-line. It is not at all unusual for people to lose sleep for a few nights when faced with navigating this major milestone in life.

And in an instance like this, even small mistakes can be costly. Big mistakes can be deadly. There is little room for errors and sloppiness.

The truth is, the real estate and the financial worlds are filled with sharks who are more than happy to take advantage of a relatively uninformed consumer. Contrary to what you may want to believe, bankers, mortgage, lenders, realtors, and even property owners are not looking out for your best interests. They are only looking after their own.

So, you owe it to yourself to educate yourself about the process, so that you can show up to the battlefield well prepared to face your opponents. Many people have done the opposite, only to pay dearly for their ignorance. You don't want to be one of them.

And this is why this book is best for you. In it, we will cover literally every nitty-gritty detail you need to be aware of - things that will give you an edge. Things that will keep you from making what could ultimately be the worst mistake of your life.

We will look at whether owning a home is a step you should take in the first place. Many people don't consider this. Depending on where you are in life, owning a home may not be the best decision. This mostly has to do with your financial health and other accompanying factors like a career choice. We will look at these in the first chapter.

We will also look at the various players in this sector that you will be dealing with. These people are compensated only when you buy and are therefore incentivized to make you spend the most that you possibly can. They are not on your side, and you need to know how you can evaluate and deal with them.

We will also walk through the list of things you need to consider about the home you will buy. Things like overall cost, closing costs, size, location, property taxes, and more, are things that you need to think about before proceeding further with matters concerning the purchase.

It is also important to note that almost everyone acquires a home through the help of a financial institution that is willing to extend credit to fund the purchase. There is a market that caters to this very need by offering mortgage products. We will look at how you can evaluate different options that exist, including the government-backed options that can cover you if you can't come up with a substantial down-payment. This knowledge is absolutely crucial.

Throughout the rest of the book, we will also look at the entire home-buying process, from selecting a real estate agent… to browsing for properties… to selecting one that fits your needs and desires… to negotiating for the best possible deal… to showing your interest by paying earnest money… to inspection… to escrow…all the way to closing the deal.

All these are crucial steps that you will need considerable guidance to navigate. And the book that you are holding right now delivers the goods.

I have gone to great pains to make sure that I cover relevant issues comprehensively without leaving out crucial matters out, all while ensuring that this book doesn't aim to turn you into a real estate expert. We are all busy people who lead lives chased by the clock. The last thing you want is to waste time trying to learn another man's craft.

That said, I am quite positive that you will learn a great deal and gain useful insights that will help you make the best home-buying decision you can possibly make without spending too much time on the matter.

I welcome you to join me on a thrilling journey of discovery in the chapters to come. I promise you won't be disappointed.

So without further ado, let's get started as soon as possible, shall we?

Please visit our website: https://easycashforhouse.com/

Like us on Facebook: https://www.facebook.com/ebraveboy

Please follow us on Instagram: http://www.instagram.com/ebraveboy/

Contents

Introduction iii

Who Is A First-Time Homebuyer? 1

Is Home Buying Best For You Right Now? 9

    Owning A Home Versus Renting 10

    The Benefits Of Owning A Home 10

    The Benefits Of Renting 17

    What Is The State Of Your Finances? 22

    What You Should Expect 30

What Type Of Home Fits Your Needs? 48

    Determining Your Most Important Factors 49

    Create A "Must Have" List 82

Your Home-Buying Check/Wish-List 84

Securing Financing 91

    What Is A Mortgage? 92

    The Different Types of Mortgages 93

    Fees Charged By Mortgage Lenders 106

    How To Shop For And Select A Mortgage Product 111

    How To Choose A Lender To Work With 116

How To Evaluate Mortgage Products 122

    Other Things To Consider 126

The Home Buying Process 141

    Step 1: Assembling The Right Team.........................141

    Step 2: Locating A Good Home Deal.........................157

    Principles To Keep In Mind 158

    Step 3: Having The Home Inspected 172

    What Will Your Inspector Be Looking For?...................... 174

    Inspection Packages To Consider.................................175

    House Inspection Checklist.. 179

    Step 4: Negotiating the deal 189

    Making Your First Offer 190

    Contingencies 197

    Step 5: Closing The Deal.. 200

Closing Costs You Should Expect 202

Closing Thoughts: Points To Keep In Mind..................... 209

Conclusion 218

Get Your Free Copy Of My Book...220

Who Is A First-Time Homebuyer?

Are you a first-time homebuyer? How do you figure?

Most people would imagine that a first-time homebuyer is someone who has never owned a home before. But this is only part of the truth. Legally speaking, there is a much more extended definition of a first-time homebuyer that you ought to be aware of. This way, you don't run the risk of missing out on the potential advantages of a first-time homebuyer, simply because your knowledge was limited.

So, here's what you need to know. You belong to the category of first time home buyers if you meet at least one of these conditions:

1. You've never owned a primary residence for at least 3 years. Please note that a primary residence is the main location that you inhabit most of the time. This can be anything: a trailer, a condo, an apartment, a boat, and so on.

   It is also worth noting that this condition only applies to one person. If you are a married couple, and only one of you meets this condition, then both of you are fully qualified as first-time homebuyers, but only if you decide to purchase a home together.

2. You are a parent who is currently single, and who only co-owned his or her previous residence with the former spouse.

3. You are a homemaker (manager of a home), who co-owned with a spouse, but then got displaced. This applies to both men and women.

4. You have owned a home before, but it was not fixed onto a permanent foundation (think mobile homes, boats, and the like), in a way that is in harmony with local regulations.

5. You have owned a home before, but it wasn't as per local or state regulations, and the cost of making it compliant would be much higher than constructing a new one.

There you have it - the definition of a first-time homebuyer, at least according to the law. Perhaps you are surprised at what you've discovered. After all, the legal definition is a far cry from the literal meaning. But the law is the law. And the government, together with lenders, will treat you accordingly.

Okay, now you may be wondering, "What is so special about being a first-time homebuyer as per the legal definition?" Is it anything significant?

Well, the truth is, there are significant advantages to being a first-time homebuyer. The government offers incentives that are designed to relax the circumstances of first-time home buyers. Therefore, you will have an easier time compared to regular home buyers.

Let's spend some time and explore what those special advantages are:

1. *Government-sponsored buyer programs*

One distinctive advantage that you, as a first-time homebuyer, may enjoy is financial assistance afforded by government-sponsored programs.

You see, many first-time home buyers find it hard to deal with the associated costs of buying a home, and the government feels obligated to help these people.

In some cases, the type of financial assistance extended is a grant aimed at helping you deal with associated costs of buying a home, such as the down payment on a home. In other cases, the assistance is aimed at helping you cover the closing costs associated with buying a home.

One such program is called **HomePath Ready Buyer Program by Fannie Mae.**

This program was launched recently in 2015 by the Federal National Mortgage Association (or Fannie Mae). The goal of this program is to assist first-time homebuyers to come up with the money required to cover closing costs.

Typically, this money is extended in the form of a rebate. A rebate is some kind of refund that is given to someone after they've made some sort of payment. In this case, the rebate is 3% of the purchasing price on the home.

This is amount is well within the range of most closing costs. If the amount ends up being insufficient, at least a huge percentage of it will have been subsidized.

However, this rebate is provided on the condition that you agree to attend a home-buying course offered by the program. Since this course costs only $75 (and is refundable once you buy the property), I perceive this to be a win-win situation for you.

The Fannie Mae program is at the federal level. Other similar programs are provided by the state and county governments. Be sure to check with your local government's housing website to discover the various programs available.

Note: *Details on what closing costs are, as well as what they typically consist of will be covered later.*

2. Tax benefits

The next class of advantages that you could enjoy by being a first-time homebuyer are the tax benefits.

To begin, as a first-time homebuyer, you are free to tap into your IRA and withdraw any amount up to $10,000, penalty-free, as long as you intend to spend the money on home related costs.

Now, since this rule applies to just one individual, it, therefore, means that a couple can withdraw up to $20,000 penalty-free. However, keep in mind that the money has to be used within 120 days before the 10% penalty becomes applicable once again.

Next, you have tax credits. A tax credit is a financial incentive that helps you minimize your tax liabilities by making deductions on your tax return. First-time homebuyers, in some states, are allowed to convert their mortgage interest payments into a federal tax credit. Texas is one such state. Check with your state housing website to find out whether there is such a provision.

3. *Federally-backed loans*

Lastly, first-time homebuyers have the advantage of qualifying for federally backed loans.

These are loans that are guaranteed by the federal government. By guaranteed, I mean that if you happen to default on them, the government will be responsible for paying the full balance.

Also, with these loans, the government has set special qualification requirements. For instance, with some of these loans, the required minimum down payment is a lot lower when compared to conventional loans. Also, the credit rating requirements are much lower than those from private lenders.

Some of the popular ones include:

- Dollar homes: This features foreclosed homes for sale by the government

- FHA loan: Some of the best programs for buyers with a weak credit rating

- VA loan: Loans requiring no downpayment that is specially designed for buyers with a military connection

- USDA loans: 100% financing for purchasing a home in rural areas

- Good Neighbor Next Door: This is a great program for first responders and educators: http://www.hudhomestore.com/Home/GNND.aspx

- Fannie and Freddie: I mentioned this earlier. I will get you conventional loans with just 3% downpayment

- Home Renovation Loans: If you wish to remodel a home, these would be ideal programs. They include FHA 203(k) loans, Energy Efficient Mortgage program, CHOICERenovation loan and HomeStyle

- State first time home buyers programs – This resource has a comprehensive list of first time home buyer programs by state: https://bit.ly/buyerprograms

This is just a teaser of these programs. I will discuss more about them later. The purpose of this teaser is to give you an understanding of the many benefits that various government bodies have to offer as you get started and why you should wear the first time homebuyer tag with pride, as it puts dollars in your pocket!

These are the three main reasons that put you at an advantageous position as a first-time homebuyer.

By taking advantage of these first-time buyer programs, you can get:

- Grants
- Save on interest
- Get help cutting down closing costs
- Benefit from deferred payments
- Possibly get loan forgiveness (where a part of the loan may be canceled upon meeting certain criteria)
- Get help paying the down payment

Obviously, all these can translate to more savings to you, hence making the home buying process less strenuous and easier for you.

With that in mind, let's move on and talk about the next most important question you ought to ask yourself.

Is Home Buying Best For You Right Now?

Owning a home is a remarkable thing to do. It is a major accomplishment in life, and a lot of people wish to achieve it someday.

But...

Is right now the best time to consider doing it?

Most people think it is. People think, "After all, isn't owning a home much better than paying rent all your life? Isn't paying rent all about making your landlord richer?"

These and many other considerations are the justifications that most of us have when we think about buying a home.

In many ways, we may be right. But, at the same time, we could be wrong.

You see, deciding to buy or not to buy a home is a complex matter. A lot has to be taken into account. You can't just cherry-pick facts and conclude that you are right.

The fact is, buying a home right now may be the right decision for some of us. But, for many of us, it could be a premature decision that might require waiting it out for a while. What's more, some of us have no business buying a home at all.

The goal of this chapter is to help you go over the various issues that you will need to consider for you to make a prudent decision over whether buying a home is a feasible idea or not. Hopefully, by the end of it, you will make a more informed decision. And the importance of doing so cannot be underestimated.

We will begin by first comparing the advantages of owning a home versus those of renting. This will help you avoid jumping into conclusions over the nature of your current situation.

Owning A Home Versus Renting

The truth of the matter is that there are advantages on both sides of the equation. Let's begin by looking at those of owning a home.

The Benefits Of Owning A Home

Owning a home is advantageous for various reasons. They include:

i) *Homes are cheaper in the long run*

This is perhaps the most attractive feature of owning a home.

Most people would wish to bring down the cost of living, and one way of doing that involves owning a home because, in the long run, you can save yourself a fortune.

To shed some light on this, let me make a simplistic comparison.

Let's say that right now, you belong to the upper-middle-class and have a good job. So conservatively speaking, you can afford to pay rent at $2,000 per month.

You are fairly convinced that your rent is cheap and that owning a home is going to be burdensome. After all, living within your means is very important, and homes in your area are very, very expensive.

But a part of your brain seems to tell you, "Not so fast, how about considering the alternative?"

You decide to establish whether, in the long run, it is beneficial to own a home instead of paying the rent. Therefore, you decide to base your comparison off a typical $2,000 a month mortgage that takes 30 years to pay off.

When you multiply the number of months in the 30 years with $2,000, you find that at the end of it all, you can easily own a $720,000 home.

How amazing! Who thought that owning such an expensive home could be possible? Such a home would no doubt be located in some of the highest quality neighborhoods in America. You've never thought of ever affording to live in one of these places, but now the math shows that it is very much possible for you.

The flip-side of it is that if you continue paying rent, you will have surrendered an equal amount to your landlord, without ever owning anything at the end of it all. In addition to that, the rental bill will keep getting handed over to you each month.

You must also not forget that the above estimates are very conservative, to say the least. It is a known fact that, as inflation and the value of properties go up, rental prices are expected to keep rising as well.

Research from [Apartment List](#) shows that rental prices have risen over the years since 1960 at a much higher rate than the average household income.

So, you could easily pay well over $1,000,000 in rent at the end of 30 years.

Obviously, this is a situation that almost no one ever wants to be in.

So, if you have the means, owning a home is definitely much better in the long run.

ii) *You can build wealth*

The pride of homeownership is certainly a satisfying one, but an even tastier side-benefit is that you can use it as a vehicle to amass wealth. And who wouldn't want that?

You see, the numbers dictate that over the long run, homes tend to appreciate in value, and at a rate that stays well ahead of inflation.

Check out the line graph below, which comes from the U.S Department of Housing and Urban Development.

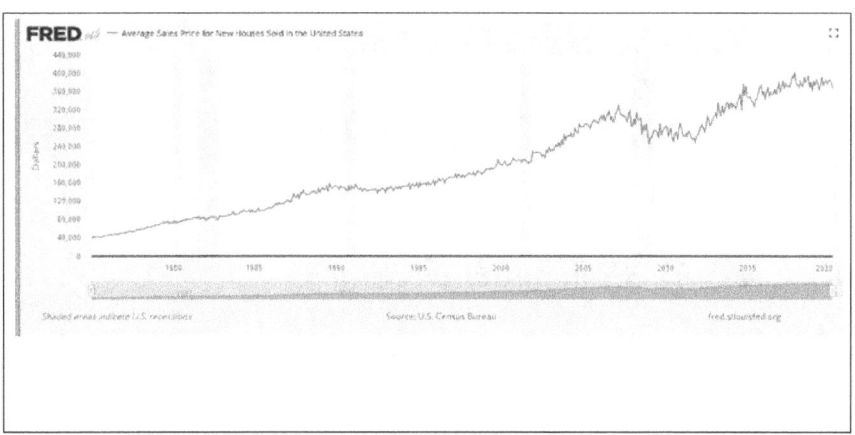

https://fred.stlouisfed.org/series/ASPNHSUS

It indicates that throughout history, home prices have always risen. Keep in mind that this data factors in the economic booms and busts that have occurred in the real estate market over the decades.

So, this shows that despite the good and the bad times, homes manage to uphold their value, and even appreciate. This qualifies a home as a valid wealth-building tool.

During your retirement years, you could decide to cash in your investment by trading down to a less expensive home and freeing up the equity in your home. You could use this money to manage your living expenses, start a business, fund your children's or grandchildren's college tuition, donate to charitable causes, and any number of things that you might want to do with your big bucks.

You can even choose to hold on to the property and pass it over to your children and grandchildren.

The bottom line is that you are less likely to go wrong by buying a home.

iii) *The freedom of ownership*

It is no secret that we all love the freedom that comes with owning our own things.

When you own something, you get to dictate your own terms. You have a say on how it should be used, how well it should be taken care of, whether you will even allow others to use it, among many things.

Simply put, ownership is bliss.

When you own your own home, you will enjoy such privileges. Perhaps you want to have a small garden in your backyard. Maybe you want to change the color of the paint. Maybe you want to install a swimming pool. Maybe you want your own privacy and prefer not to have anyone on the premises. Maybe this maybe that. The options are just limitless.

The one problem with renting is that your residence is forever the property of your landlord. And as such, the landlord gets to dictate the terms. Much of the time, you don't have a say over anything.

There have been many instances where tenants have complained over the poor maintenance of property from tightwad landlords. Check out the controversial story of Leona Helmsley, who was so notorious in her days, that tenants even took her to court. They even had a name for her, "The Queen of Mean."

If you wish to avoid these inconveniences, then ownership may be perfect for you.

iv)   *Tax advantages*

Homeownership is such an important thing in the U.S, and the government even provides incentives to encourage people to acquire homes. One such incentive is the law that makes associated homeownership costs tax-deductible.

One such cost is mortgage payments. Other costs that are tax-deductible include closing costs and property taxes. All these combined can greatly reduce your tax burden.

Even home equity loans, which are a better alternative to expensive credit card debt, are tax-deductible. How cool is that? You not only pay less interest, you also get tax advantages for taking them.

What's more, if you decide to sell your home later in the future, you can keep the profits without owing capital gains tax if they amount to less than $250,000. If you are married, you are allowed to keep up to $500,000 of the profits, free of capital gains tax.

v)   *It's a forced savings and investment plan*

Saving is a good financial habit. Investing is another close second. We all know that we should do these basic things, but for some reason, the vast majority of us lack the discipline to do them.

CNBC reports that the vast majority of Americans (50%) have nothing saved for retirement. It is reported that only a paltry 15% of Americans have $10,000 kept aside in savings.

Why do we have such shocking numbers? It has to do with the freedom that we have in making choices with our money.

The freedom that we have with choosing how we spend our own money many times works against us. We fail to follow simple rules that will lead to a healthier financial future. That is, unless we are forced to do so, in a way.

And that is what homeownership really amounts to. Since you are obligated to pay your mortgage or get kicked out to the street and lose your home, you are likely to fight tooth and nail to do it.

And while you are at it, you are not only stashing away thousands of dollars for the future; you are also investing in an asset that is a proven investment tool. So you are essentially forced to get the best of both worlds.

Later on in life, you can cash in your investment and do whatever you wish to do with it.

If you belong to the category of people who earn a good living but can't bring yourself to have the discipline to save and invest, the least you can do is purchase a home. It's better than having nothing in the end.

Now, let us look at the other end of the spectrum – renting.

The Benefits Of Renting

Renting has its perks too. Some of them include:

i) *Less hustle in finding one*

If there is one sure thing about finding a home, no matter how knowledgeable you may be about it, it's that it takes a lot of time and hard work.

There are many things involved in the process. There is checking your financial health. Then there is consulting with lenders. There's browsing the market, finding a realtor to educate you about the market and finding deals, negotiating deals, dealing with paperwork. Blah blah blah. And let's not even talk about the money involved while all this craziness is going on.

To be honest, it's an exhaustive process that can easily get under the nerves of even the most patient person.

Truth be said, renting is a lot easier. If you have an idea of what you want and your monthly budget. A day or two of browsing the market usually turns up valuable results. You sign some paperwork involving the details of your lease, and you're done; the next thing you do, is simply moving in.

And in a time-strapped world where people are trying to get things done in as little time as possible with little overhead, I have to say the option of renting certainly sounds very appealing to many.

Sure, it may appear to be expensive in the long run, but there are ways to offset the risk involved if one has a tremendous ability to generate a good income.

Buying a home often involves a lot, but sometimes bad things happen, and if you are not keen on the details, you can easily get ripped off in a bad deal. Hopefully, this book will help you avoid such a scenario.

ii) *Less work in upkeep*

Not only does the home-buying process take a great toll on your time and finances, the work involved afterward in maintaining it can also be pretty exhausting.

There will be trouble with mowing the lawn, repairing leaky roofs, fixing blocked toilets, trimming the hedge, and much, much more. This means that your weekends will be pretty busy. You can kiss a good number of picnics goodbye. If you can't take on these tasks, then you will have to pay someone to do them for you.

You see, some neighborhoods have very strict standards regarding how well-kept the homes in it should be so you can't just shrug your shoulders and turn a blind eye. And needless to say, more money out of your pocket, especially after investing a large sum can be difficult. It can bring you close to financial disaster.

Renting involves much less headache in comparison. For one thing, the property you live in belongs to your landlord, and so, he or she is responsible for any emerging costs that might arise. All you have to do is pay your rent and pay for some basic services like garbage collection or HOA, depending on the terms of the lease. The rest, you simply live it to him or her.

This is a great relief for those of us who work in cities, and in professions that involve long hours and a lot of work. Often, we need to work 6 to 7 days a week, and can't afford even a weekend to mow the lawn.

If you belong to this category, then you might determine that renting is a better fit for your lifestyle (and perhaps a lot cheaper), when compared to owning your own home.

iii) *You are more flexible*

Flexibility in today's world has become a valuable thing to have.

You might be in a career that has great prospects for advancing, but that requires you to travel a lot. Or your boss might consider relocating you to head a new office located in some other part of the world or country.

In today's faced-paced world of business, characterized by globalization and the influence of technology, such developments are considered to be the norm rather than the exception. And since many people are employees in these businesses, it is not unusual to receive such requests from employers.

This means that a permanent residence can end up hurting you, more than it will ever do you good. If you buy a home and suddenly have to move a few months later, you are almost sure to lose money even in a stable, rising market.

This is because it takes time, preferably at least 3 years for you to even breakeven on your original investment, let alone make any profit whatsoever – of course, unless yours was a fixer upper that you can sell immediately you've upgraded it. And if you are in a hurry to sell, then you will have to quote below market value for you to attract buyers and sell quickly.

This can be financially devastating, especially considering that money isn't the most easily renewable resource.

If you are in a situation whereby flexibility is more of a requirement rather than a luxury, then homeownership is a risky undertaking. Renting is a much better fit since you can move around as much as you need without committing vast financial resources.

iv)   *More money to invest in other vehicles*

With all the hype going around about the need to own a home, and its long-term benefits, it can start to feel like you may be missing on an important investment opportunity if you don't get a home as early as possible.

The pressure tends to build up, especially in a runaway real estate market, when property prices start making headlines almost daily.

The important thing is to not get suckered by this. The truth is, real estate isn't the only investment vehicle that is worth putting your money in. You can invest in your own business, stocks, bonds, Real Estate Investment Trusts (or REITs), and many other sound investment vehicles.

Even simply investing in your own career has been known to pay the highest returns. If you move to the top of your chosen vocation, you can easily earn enough money to purchase a home in cash in later years.

And if you rent, you will have more disposable income to purchase other investments. But, if you put a lot of your own money in one investment that also happens to weigh you down, you will likely expose your portfolio to more risk than might be necessary.

Okay, at this point, you probably now understand that homeownership isn't the Holy Grail and should only be considered if circumstances show that the upside outweighs the downside. Moving on, we will talk about how you can analyze your financial health to make sure that you are, in fact, ready to purchase your first home without leading to disaster.

What Is The State Of Your Finances?

Heading out to take a mortgage to finance the purchase of a home without considering the state of your financial health is a recipe for disaster. If it happens (as is often the case), that the state of your finances is less than impressive, then you may be in for a rude awakening down the road.

Take the example of Matt - a fairly successful lawyer at one of the most prestigious law firms in New York.

He inhabits the metropolitan area, which is home to other successful professionals like him; people like doctors, stockbrokers, hedge fund managers, executives of public corporations, and so on.

Matt's life wasn't always like this. He comes from a lower-middle-class background. Many are the times when he and his parents struggled just to get by in life. Money wasn't always easy to come by.

They weren't exactly poor, but they struggled financially to stay afloat. His parents always urged him to work very hard so that he would one day live a more comfortable life in the more "upscale neighborhoods." Matt heeded his parents' advice and worked very hard.

Today, Matt is not just proud to be a member of this "exclusive group"; he is ecstatic. He is convinced that he and his neighbors have a lot in common. He will copy their consumption habits from choice of home, to standard of clothing, to meals, and everything else that can be bought with money.

Matt feels that he doesn't need to budget for anything. He's never felt the need to. He thinks that it is a time-wasting activity that only needs to be done by people who are strapped for cash.

If he wants something, he will have it in one way or another. If the cash isn't in hand, he will just acquire the item on credit with his American Express Platinum card. He has others from Diners Club, Saks Fifth Avenue, Brooks Brothers, and Nordstrom.

Quite recently, some real estate agents and mortgage brokers visited his firm to advertise homes had just been completed in the Upper East Side, and that were up for grabs. The marketers were dangling the prospects of easy homeownership with very little money down.

His friends were very impressed by the opportunity and quickly signed up. Matt, being the crowd follower that he is, thought, "Why Not? If my friends can afford it, I surely can. I can't pass up this opportunity up and be left behind." In the state of euphoria, he quickly signed on the dotted lines in the forms that they were provided with. A month later, Matt moved into his new home, along with his wife and three children.

It turns out that Matt, who had never analyzed his finances a day in his life was in for real trouble. Not only had he underestimated the size of his credit card debt, but he had also failed to calculate just how much the monthly costs of owning the home would be.

Soon, his debts were spiraling out of control. Owning a home in a prestigious neighborhood was supposed to be a joy to him and his family. Now, it was turning out to be very painful. Matt became depressed and soon had to consult with a psychiatrist who recommended that he seeks the services of a financial advisor.

After carefully assessing his situation, Matt's advisor recommended that he sell some of his assets and move to a cheaper rental apartment, at least until his financial situation improved.

Many people are like Matt. They move too quickly without considering the facts. Later on, they have to deal with a situation that is far much worse than they had expected.

If you don't want homeownership to be devastating, you better know how to analyze your finances to determine whether you are in fact ready. Let's look at some ways that you can do that yourself.

i) *Budget*

Yes, one of the most critical steps to undertake when considering buying a home is to draw up a budget. A budget keeps track of all the money that comes in and goes out, as well as what is saved.

It's quite simple when you think of it, and many people agree that having one is a good idea. But Debt.com once reported from a survey, that 1 in 3 Americans don't have a budget.

But why is a budget so crucial?

Because it helps you look realistically at your financial situation. It helps you determine whether the expenses of your home fit in the equation. For instance, if you estimate that your mortgage plus costs like insurance, repairs, and property taxes will amount to about $1200 per month, then you might find that the amount is easily swappable with your rent.

A budget also helps you estimate how expensive your home can be. It doesn't you no good to take out a mortgage on a home that your budget can't handle.

So how do you prepare a budget anyway? Here are some steps that you can follow.

Step 1: Collect all your financial documents

The first step is to collect every paperwork at your disposal that has to do with money. By this, I mean documents that might indicate your income or spending.

Some documents that you might consider include the following:

- Utility bills
- Brokerage statements
- Bank account statements
- Paystubs
- Tax statements
- Credit card bills
- Receipts
- And so on

The goal is to track all your living expenses as well as your income. I recommend that you get in the habit of keeping all financial documents that you receive whenever you can. If you do so, for a couple of months, you will get a good idea of your income and spending patterns. That information is worth its weight in gold.

Step 2: Determine how much you earn

How much do you bring in?

If you are employed, that is easy to determine. You just take a look at your take-home (net) pay from your paystub.

If you are self-employed or run a business, then you will have to crunch the numbers and determine an average. Tally up your income for say, six months or so. Get the mean of that figure, and you have an idea of what you make in a typical month.

You can get an accountant to help you out with this. Issues concerning business income and taxation can get quite complex. Unless you are an accounting professional yourself, getting the help of someone skilled in these matters in your best option.

Step 3: Determine how much you spend.

How much goes out?

A good place to start is the pile of financial statements that you have in hand. These statements can show you where most of the money you make goes. Once you get these basic expenses down, you'll have to work out the rest, which are not so obvious.

It helps to create a detailed list of every expense you note. An even better idea is to break them up to categories. Generally, expenses fall into three categories, namely:

1. Fixed expenses

These are the basic expenses that tend to remain the same each month. Think of things like rent, car payments, student loan payments, insurance, and so on.

Most of the time, these are things that you can't do without or would have to change your standard of living to affect them drastically. These changes can have a profound impact on your financial bottom-line.

For instance, getting rid of your car and taking public transport can take off a huge burden.

2. Flexible expenses.

Then there is the category of flexible expenses.

As the name suggests, these are expenses that tend to vary each month that passes. Items that belong to this list include utilities, food, groceries, and so on.

3. Discretionary expenses.

Lastly, you have discretionary expenses.

These are expenses that exist out of your own free will. You can choose to have or not have them because they represent luxuries.

Items to place here include vacations, meals at restaurants, tickets to movies, and so on.

These expenses provide some room to cut back because they can easily be eliminated or significantly reduced.

Step 4: Tally both sides and find the difference

Once you've gotten both your expenses and income down, list them side by side and get the total on both sides.

The idea is to find out just how much you bring in and compare that amount to what you spend. Ideally, your expenses should be well below what you earn. If that appears to be the case as per the document in front of you then you are on the right track.

Purchasing a home will be a lot easier for you since you will have money to stash away into savings, and can withstand a sudden change in finances.

What You Should Expect

If you have bothered to go through the steps I have just laid out, then there are some basic outcomes that you should expect. Each outcome will imply something different.

a)   You find that your spending is too high

This is the likely outcome for most people. It is not at all unusual for people to spend all or more than what they earn.

Perhaps you didn't realize that you spend close to $500 on lunch at restaurants. Or you discover that your car is really swallowing you alive through its sizeable monthly payments.

In any event, if your budget indicates that you are spending well beyond your means, then you should sense some trouble. You will need to adjust your finances and get things in order before you can consider the idea of buying a home.

The obvious thing is to cut back on your expenses. Find areas where you can tighten things up a little, or even eliminate altogether. For instance, you can choose to carry packed lunch to work and avoid eating out. You could also choose to move to a cheaper house so that rent costs you less.

b)   *You find that you are doing well*

If you tend to be much disciplined when it comes to matters concerning your finances, then you might find yourself in this category.

You spend well within your means, and you have plenty left to put aside for retirement and savings. If this is the case, then the decision to buy a home may be a wise thing to do, provided other considerations seem to be in favor of doing so.

But how do you even determine that you belong in this enviable position in the first place?

There is a simple criterion that you can use.

If you find that you manage to save at least 20% of your income, then you are definitely on the right track.

This number comes from the well understood 50:30:20 rule that was popularized by the book, "All Your Worth: The Ultimate Lifetime Money Plan by Senator Elizabeth Warren.

According to the rule, you should allocate 50% of your income to basic needs. 30% of it ought to go into expenses that are more discretionary and luxuries. Lastly, the remaining 20% is meant to go into saving.

If you are able to follow this rule, then you can consider yourself to be on the right track financially. This should be your target if you haven't yet met this standard.

c)   *You save quite a lot*

The last scenario involves those who save well beyond the expected threshold.

If you belong to this group, congratulations because you are a true outlier -few people manage to meet this very high standard.

If you fall into this category, you may be well on your way to build wealth or are already wealthy. For you, purchasing a home may not hurt your bottom-line. You may even extend yourself a bit and buy a more expensive home.

Still, you will need to watch your finances carefully and consider other factors that I talk about later in this chapter to ensure that you don't commit a serious error that throws you off-track.

Having discussed the subject of budgeting extensively, it helps to know that there are tools out there that can make the job of preparing a sound and comprehensive budget a lot less messy. After all, dealing with a mountain of paperwork can get tedious. And in this digital era, you should save yourself such inconveniences whenever you can.

These tools include:

- MS Excel – MS Excel is the world's most popular spreadsheet application. There are many people out there who have created reliable templates to help you with the task of putting together a household budget. And they are all free. My favorite one comes from Vertex42. However, there are many other vendors, and all you need to perform is a simple Google search.

- Free apps – You also have the option of free apps that you can install, and that can help organize all your finances conveniently from the comfort of your smartphone. Some good ones are: Mint, Pocketguard, You Need A Budget (YNAB), Wally, Goodbudget.

That said, let's look at the next method of evaluating your fiscal stability.

ii) *Emergency Fund*

We have already talked at length about how purchasing a home can rock your financial boat, even if you have enjoyed financial stability for quite some time. You owe it to yourself to make plans to make sure that owning a home will not cause you many sleepless nights should unexpected expenses arise.

So besides having a well-thought-out budget, you also need to make sure that you have a well-funded emergency fund.

An emergency fund is exactly what it sounds. It is a cash reserve that you keep on the side, which is meant to take care of sudden and unexpected expenses.

You see, anything can happen the moment you move into your exciting new home. You could suddenly lose your job, a parent can get seriously ill, your car may break down, or the roof of your house may need repair.

All these are huge expenses that can hit anyone at any time. You haven't budgeted for them, so they are not very easy to take care of without going into debt (often high-interest credit card debt). And needless to say, debt is usually not good for your finances.

This is why having this kind of fund in place is always a good thing to do. It keeps you from getting into trouble by providing a much-needed financial cushion- unless, of course, your situation takes a turn for the worst.

How much should you have in this account?

Financial experts recommend that you set aside anywhere between 3 to 6 months' worth of expenses. If your income pattern is unpredictable (if you are self-employed, for instance), having this fund is especially important. The six months threshold is considered a minimum threshold.

And what about the storage location? Should you just put this money anywhere you wish? Of course not. You want to the money to be in a place where you can easily access it when needed. This means that storing it in areas where high returns are expected, and high penalties are charged for early withdrawals, is a very bad idea.

High yield savings accounts are considered to provide the best features. They won't make you a fortune, but at least you can be sure that you will access the money whenever you need it. And if the bank goes belly up, you can fully expect that your money will be safe because the federal government insures these accounts up to $250,000.

iii) Credit Score

If you are like most people, you will definitely need to borrow to finance the purchase of your home. This means that a third party, such as a bank, a mortgage lender, or some other financial institution, will have to step in.

For this reason, it is good to make sure that you have a good credit score. If you've never heard of it, a credit score is a three-digit number that is used to indicate your creditworthiness.

Keep in mind that most lenders would be willing to do business with you as long as they confident that you will pay back the money that you owe along with interest and in good time. A credit score is used to quantify your ability to do this.

A high credit score means that you pose less risk to the lender. If this is the case, then lenders are more than willing to extend a line of credit to you. What's more, they are willing to provide attractive terms. For instance, you will qualify for a higher amount and with competitive rates.

A low or even poor credit score implies the opposite. A lender perceives you as a risky borrower. He or she is basically taking chances with you as to whether you will pay back the money or not. This works to your disadvantage. Lenders will typically be less willing to extend credit to you, which means that you will have fewer options in the credit markets. What's more, the lenders that will be willing to lend to you will offer a lower amount and with higher interest. This means that taking a loan with them ends up being painful and burdensome since you will be working harder to keep up with high-interest payments.

So you see, it is in your best interest to make sure that you have a better than average credit score. It's going to make your life a whole lot easier when it comes to owning your own home.

You've understood the importance of having a good credit score. So how do you go about making sure that that you are on the right track? Good question.

First, it helps to know exactly what counts for a good credit score. At the moment, most lenders rely on two popular models to calculate your credit score. These models are from two companies FICO (Fair Isaac Corporation) and Vantage.

The models used by these two companies generate a three-digit figure that ranges from 300 to 850. The higher you rank on this scale, the better your credit score is.

Check out the table below to understand what each category of score means to a typical financial institution that is looking to lend you money for anything.

FICO SCORE		VANTAGE SCORE	
Range	Classification	Range	Classification
300 – 579	Very Poor	300 – 499	Very Poor
580 – 669	Fair	500 – 600	Poor
670 – 739	Good	601 – 660	Fair
740 – 799	Very Good	661 – 780	Good
800 – 850	Exceptional	781 – 850	Excellent

The financial industry works with numbers, and the table above shows how they interpret you. They don't care that you are smart, good-looking, well dressed, or any physically observable qualities. All they want to know is whether you are a risky borrower who is likely to default on his/her loan or make late payments.

How do you know where you rank on this scale? Well, the good news is that you can get access to this data for free. In the past, you had to pay to know your credit score, but the world has moved on. Times are better now, and some apps will give you access to your credit score for free. You can choose any one of them.

They include:

- [Credit Sesame](#)
- [Mint Money Manager](#)
- [Credit Karma](#)
- [TransUnion](#)
- [Experian](#)

You can request a free credit report from the three major credit reporting companies (Equifax, Experian, and TransUnion) from https://www.annualcreditreport.com.

Okay, so let's say that you've downloaded and signed up to one of these tools and now have an idea of what your credit score looks like. If it's bad, then you will have to forgo the option of buying a home for at least a few years until you can get your financial outlook in order. It's not rocket science to figure out this part.

And what if you find that your credit score isn't very bad, but offers room for improvement? If so, then you'll be happy to know that there are steps you can take to improve your credit score so that you are more attractive in the eyes of lenders.

You see, your credit score is generated by applying a proprietary algorithm to data generated by your credit reports.

And, just like any algorithm, there are certain things you can do to affect the outcome it produces.

Let's talk about what some of those things are:

1. *Pay your bills on time*

The first thing you can do to make sure that you affect your credit score is affected positively is to make sure that your bills are paid on time.

And by bills, we are not just talking about credit card bills and auto loans. All trackable bills such as utilities, rent, phone bills, student loans, and so on are factored in as well.

Bankers figure that past performance is a good predictor of the future. So if you have a spotless record of making payments on time with few or no late payments in between, then you are a good candidate for being lent to.

2. *Pay off your debt*

Another way that you can improve your credit score is by paying off whatever debt you may have.

This is important because it helps reduce what bankers refer to as credit utilization rate. Credit utilization rate is a ratio that quantifies how much you tend to extend yourself, given your credit limit. It is calculated by dividing your outstanding debt balances by your credit limit.

For instance, if you have a credit limit of $10,000, and you happen to take $2,000 in debt, then your credit utilization rate is 20%. For a good credit score, you need to make sure that your rate is at 30% or lower.

One way of achieving this is paying off whatever debt you may have, and maintaining as low a balance as you possibly can.

3. Avoid taking on unnecessary debt, especially revolving debt

If you can avoid borrowing, then do so.

This is especially true when it comes to what is known as revolving debt. Revolving debt is debt that makes money available to you up to a certain limit. You are then required to pay whatever is on balance. Once you pay off all or part of the debt, an equal amount is made available for use.

Revolving debt is typically used by individuals and companies to smooth out unstable cash-flows and provide the much-needed liquidity.

Usually, with revolving debt, you only need to pay the minimum amount required by the lender. Often, this is usually just the fee. Once you do that, the balance can always be carried forward. Therefore, revolving debt doesn't obligate you to pay it by a certain date.

A good example of a well-known type of revolving debt is credit card debt.

Revolving debt usually has a negative impact on your credit score, because most people never use them responsibly. It is not at all unusual for people to rack up huge credit card balances that remain unpaid for years. Most people accomplish this feat pay paying just the minimum amount required by the lender.

Even more, revolving debt increases your credit utilization rate, which, as we have already established, hurts your score.

Therefore take as little revolving debt as you can. It is much better to take installment loans, which require you to pay off a certain amount each month with interest. Such loans reflect more responsible use of credit and have a much better effect on your credit score.

4. Avoid closing out unused accounts

If you have managed to take several credit cards and have paid off the balance in quite a number of them, it is smart to avoid closing them.

This is because each of these cards has its own limits; therefore, extending your overall credit card limit. And if the balance on these cards is small or even nonexistent, then it means that your credit utilization rate is even lower, which tends to work in your favor.

I am not encouraging you to get as many credit cards as you possibly can. This is foolhardy because hard credit inquiries also affect your score as well. This is a strategy that works in your favor, only if you had already taken several credit cards before.

5. Check for inaccuracies in reports or negotiate

It also helps to check the actual credit reports from the relevant reporting institutions such as Transunion, Equifax, and Experian.

Often, you might find some inaccuracies that can be corrected and result in a much better outcome. For instance, you might find that your credit is being tracked from the wrong accounts (perhaps someone else's).

Or, you might find that your credit history is being affected by a few late payments that are outnumbered by an almost spotless record. You can negotiate for much better treatment from the reporting institution if they find that your claims make sense.

For this reason, it is always a good habit to check your credit reports from time to time to verify their accuracy. Errors can and do happen, and they can negatively affect your score.

Your credit score is very important in determining how favorably lenders will act towards you. This is why we have spent quite some time discussing it. It is a significant input that can affect your quest to get a home.

Let us move on and discuss some other merit that you can use to assess your financial situation.

iv) *Debt to Income Ratio*

Also of importance is what is called a Debt to Income ratio (DTI).

This is a metric that measures your overall indebtedness. It measures just how much income you generate to serve your existing debts.

If you have too much debt relative to your gross income, your DTI ratio will be high, and lenders will think twice before lending you money. Or if they do so, they will have to mitigate risk by charging high risk and making less money available.

DTI ratio can be calculated as follows:

$$\text{DTI ratio} = \frac{\text{Total monthly debt payments}}{\text{Total monthly gross income}} \times 100\%$$

Generally, the lower the ratio, the better. Lenders prefer a ceiling figure of 43%. This means that 43% is the upper limit to which a lender will consider before even qualifying you for a mortgage loan. Anything beyond that is highly risky and dangerous for both parties.

However, most lenders prefer to see a number well within 36% or below it. This indicates that you are not too overstretched and can properly service the mortgage payments.

So do your math. What does your DTI ratio reveal? Are you too much into debt? If so, then you might consider increasing your income (such as by taking a second job), or paying off your debt. Both of these adjustments will reduce your DTI ration and make you more qualified for a mortgage loan.

v) Savings

You also want to consider how much you have in savings.

We have just talked about the importance of having an emergency fund. This is different. I am talking about savings that are purely meant for a project, such as purchasing a home.

Remember, for you to buy a home, you will typically require to put down a deposit first, then borrow the rest from a lender. The generally accepted rule is that you have up to 20% of the cost down. You can't afford that money if you are broke.

Some mortgage arrangements require that you put down much less, but then you may have to take a Private Mortgage Insurance. What's more, you may have to pay significantly more interest.

And keep in mind that we haven't factored in closing costs, which can add to the financial burden.

So, if you don't have enough money put aside in savings, it is a bad sign. It is a sign that you are not ready yet. Purchasing a home is a drain by itself, and the last thing you want to do is to dig yourself into a deeper hole.

If you try to buy a home without making sure that you have saved enough to take care of the process, then you may be putting yourself in a position where you end up resenting the whole decision of buying a home.

So check your reserves. How much do you have saved? If you hope to own a $200,000 home someday, make sure you have close to $50,000 in savings. If you don't, you are probably not ready and should take some more time to get in proper shape.

This is just a rough estimate; you will have to do some work to determine how much of a home you can afford (as we will see in a later chapter). But, most people who want to buy a home have a rough idea of how much home they can afford. Use that rough estimate as a guideline.

Given what we've talked about so far, you should have a pretty good idea as to whether buying a home is right for you. The depth to which we have gone into various matters might seem overkill, but I promise that it is all worth it.

Buying a home is a significant financial commitment. There is little room for error. The last thing you want to do is make a rash decision, only to end up regretting later. Therefore, being thorough is a pretty smart thing to do.

Perhaps you've found that it is better to rent now and buy later. Maybe you've discovered that you are better off never owning a home at all.

Or, if you are among the few who are in a good position, you might have discovered that the most important factors are in your favor and that owning a home is quite advantageous to you right now.

If so, congratulations. I invite you to join me in the next chapter, where you will go through the process of identifying the right type of home for you. See you there.

What Type Of Home Fits Your Needs?

Now that you have fully established whether buying a home is right for you, it is time that you considered the next most important factor – the type of home that you need.

It is important to think of this beforehand so that you show up to the marketplace, having considered everything that is vital. This way, you will not fall to the whims of high-pressure sales tactics of the market participants.

Remember, you owe it to yourself to look out for your best interests. This is a major financial decision in your life. You cannot let sloppiness or the desire to move faster cloud your better judgment.

Many professionals in the industry are interested in taking home the biggest check. And they will cash in on naivety of anyone who hasn't done their homework. You don't want to be the person who gets taken advantage of simply because you didn't perform your due diligence.

That said, in this chapter, we are going to look extensively at the various factors that should affect your decision to buy a particular. Each factor should be evaluated based on your own situation. There is no one-size-fits-all criteria.

Of course, you will have to relax your rigidity on some factors, but overall, a well-defined criteria will translate to a much better decision.

So let's get started.

Determining Your Most Important Factors

1. *The community*

One of the first and most important factors to consider when choosing a home is the community around it.

What type of community do you want to belong in? It can't be the same for all of us. We all have different tastes and preferences. We have varying levels of income and occupational status. You may be married or single. You may be stationary or a business-traveler.

So, you have to pick your community based on what is best for you.

Let's say that you belong to the upper-middle-class of society and want your lifestyle and home to reflect that. Then you will be better off looking for areas with high concentrations of people like you.

If you are among the few truly privileged persons in society (read loaded), then you obviously have a vested interest in interacting with people in your cohort. Browsing the local paper for listings on the most exclusive areas will guide to the community that you will most likely identify with.

Maybe you are retired and would wish to relate with people like you and participate in common interests and activities. Find an area that is known to have large concentrations of recently retired persons.

I hope you get the idea. It's all about locating a community that you will have a sense of belonging - one that will not leave you feeling like an outcast. And, more importantly, one that will not indulge you in commitments that you are barely interested in.

For instance, I happen to belong to the young and ambitious category. And the community I live suits my taste. I live close to the city, where I easily interact with the young and energetic. Our incomes also seem to coincide, so we engage in essentially the same activities. We consume at a level that seems to be the same among us.

Quite often, the apartments that I live in contain young people who live fairly private and career-oriented lives. It is not at all unusual for weeks to go by without meeting someone who lives next door. And it's all fine with me. Your case may be different.

There are some steps you can take to identify the ideal community. Here are some ideas to try:

- Purchase the local paper: What is the tone in the content? Who does it seem to aim? Is it you? What issues does it cover? Are they of any particular interest to you?

- Visit the area and try to get a feel for it. Stop by the mall, greet people at the supermarket, and the grocery store. Do you seem to connect? What can they tell you about the area? How long have they lived in the area? What do they like about it? What do they dislike about it? Where do they work? The locals can often tell you a lot about the area.

- Talk to your agent. He or she has more experience selling homes in the area. You can get insights from him/her about the characteristics of the neighborhood.

- Visit the website of The Chamber Of Commerce website. It is jam-packed with information about the income and population characteristics of an area or zip-code. This information can reveal a lot about a neighborhood.

You will undoubtedly end up having a sense of commitment to your community, so take the time to do your research on this one.

2. *Quality of the neighborhood*

Besides the community, you also want to reside in a quality neighborhood. While the community represents the bigger picture of your residential area and its characteristics, the neighborhood is more specific and refined.

The best way to evaluate a neighborhood is to drive around it and take note of what you see. Some things to keep in mind as you do this include:

- The number of sale signs. How many of them can you spot? A lot of homes going on sale could indicate that the market for property in the area is hot. This could be a good or bad sign, depending on how you look at it and who you ask. Just check with your real estate agent and the locals to find out whether people are flowing in or moving out and the possible explanation for that.

- What is the quality of the homes in the area? Are they well taken care of? Are they in a deplorable state and need a lot of repairs. Are they made of quality materials?

- How uniform are the properties in the area? Are they custom made or do they have similar characteristics. What about lot sizes and square footage?

Note: It is better to pick a neighborhood with homes that appear to be similar. If a home seems to stand out too much, it probably doesn't sell fast enough. And the chances of you getting a bad deal by getting ripped off are very high. People who are interested in a big house will not look for them in small neighborhoods. And people who look for small homes will not have an appetite or the means for a big house. These are important things to keep in mind if you ever hope to sell the home someday.

- What seems to be the lifestyle of the people in the neighborhood? Do they contain young families with kids? Or do you sense the presence of more established families with grown-up kids? Check out the make of motor vehicles in the driveways to get a sense of income and consumption habits. **(People tend to consume at a level that is similar to those around them.)**

- What about transport facilities. Is the area serviced by public transport? Are you interested in public means, or do you always use your private means of transportation?

- What about security? Do you see graffiti on the walls? What is the crime rate in the area? Are there facilities to take care of security matters? Visit the local police station and get data or the level of incidence of crime in the area, and the nature of it.

- What is the level of pollution in the area? Do you sense a lot of noise from cars, industries, factories, trains and so on? Do you have a problem with that? What about waste management? Is the area littered with solid waste?

Follow this list and decide for yourself whether you like what you see. You can add items as you wish, but the above should cover most of what is important. Do you see yourself living in harmony and peace with what you have uncovered? If not, keep searching.

3. The location

The importance of location is also significant. Where your house is located will affect its price and its future resale value.

The first thing you want to keep in mind with regards to location is accessibility. Do you wish to have a home that is conveniently located and accessible? If you are retired, this may not be important, but if you are still young and working, then you want to make sure that your home is accessible.

How far is it from major access roads? The farther it is, the less desirable it will be. Most people want a home that will enable them to access roads easily and get to work on time. You might be able to get a lower price for a house that violates this rule, but selling it will be a major hassle.

Preferably, you want your home to be accessible via multiple means; therefore, if multiple roads lead to your neighborhood, the better.

And what about proximity to an urban area? Homes that are close to an urban area are built on land that tends to be more valuable. What's more, land around urban areas shrinks pretty quickly, and soon enough, there isn't any available. A home situated in an area like this is highly desirable. It will go for more money but will be an easy sell and, at perhaps a greater price, due to the rapid appreciation of the land under it.

You also want to consider proximity to major roads, hospitals, factories, and fire stations. Areas like these typically have a lot of noise, which makes them less desirable. You will get a house at a lower price, but then you have to put up with noisiness. Most people know this and won't be willing to buy it later on.

Don't forget to consider the presence of restaurants, grocery stores, as well as shopping centers. These are areas where people frequently visit, and most would prefer that they stay within reach. You don't want to pick a house that is located too far away from these facilities.

4. *The resale value*

Are you planning on inhabiting your house for the rest of your life? Or are you planning on moving to a different location someday?

The data indicates that most people, especially first time home buyers, barely stay in one home for more than seven years. Do you think that this sounds a lot like you?

If so, then you definitely want to pick a home that has great resale value. Homes that tend to have great resale value are those that are in good condition, and that happen to be located in high-quality neighborhoods.

If a home is well-maintained by its inhabitants and is located in a neighborhood that has a great reputation and potential, then such a house never stays in the market for long. People tend to grab it within days after it hits the market.

Also, these are the homes that tend to appreciate, even when the real estate market isn't doing so well. In other words, these are the homes that you want to buy if you hope to get a great resale value in a short period.

The trouble is, finding these homes isn't easy. You will have to carry out considerable research to locate homes like these. This can take a huge toll on your job performance since you will have to dedicate a significant amount of time resources to find them.

If you have little time to do this kind of homework, then you will need to work with professionals. Find some of the best real estate agents in the area that have an excellent track record of predicting future home values. Walk into any major real estate firm and ask for their top guns. They can help you find what you are looking for, and with little work.

You might have to pay them more money because they are good at what they do, but you will make more in the long run.

5. *Condition*

This is also important. What condition are you comfortable with?

You can buy a home at a considerable bargain price if you happen to find it in subpar condition. If you know what you are doing, then this can be a great thing to consider. However, most people are not familiar with the game in real estate and are better off looking for a house that is in tip-top (move-in ready) condition.

So which way should you go? The answer depends on the value you place on your time and familiarity with another person's work.

If you are really busy and generally find that time spent outside your main job doesn't equate to more money, then you shouldn't gamble with such a situation. Just select a home that is in good condition and move in.

Building and fixing homes can get tricky and dirty. There are many details involved, and rip-offs abound in the business. Rookies often make costly mistakes. It is not unusual to end up spending more money fixing up a home than you had initially anticipated.

If you are self-employed and an enterprising type who doesn't mind managing details in construction, then perhaps you are better off playing this kind of game. But for most people, it tends to be more trouble than it is truly worth. It can be dangerous and detrimental to your financial stability.

6. *The needs of your family*

The needs of your family also need to be put into perspective.

How big is it? How many children do you have? Do you hope to get more? Are you planning on buying your children cars in the future? Do you think it is important to have a swimming pool installed?

And what about your parents and grandparents - do you hope to live with them, or host them someday?

The reason it is important to consider these factors is that they help determine the size of the house you will need to select. The more the demands of your family, the roomier your house will need to be. So consider your situation and select accordingly.

7. Type.

Then there is the issue of type. What type of house do you have in mind? Type, in this instance, refers to the structure (or form) that the house takes.

Let's explore some popular types of homes that you are likely to find on the market.

i)   *Single-family and multi-family homes*

Are you planning on moving in with just your own family, or are you planning to have some room left to rent out to other people?

Answering that question can influence which of the two you are going to pick.

So which one will it be?

As the name suggests, a single-family home is built to accommodate just one family. It exists as just one unit. Most people are likely to go with this option.

A multi-family home, on the other hand, is designed to accommodate more than one family. This can be the perfect option for you if you hope to generate some rental income.

Multi-family homes are typically made of multiple floors and can be referred to as duplex (where there are two units) or triplex (where the units are three).

ii) *Ranch-style*

This type of home was, at one point, the most popular design in America. Today, you will likely find less of it.

A ranch-style home is characterized by a low roof that also happens to be long. The house is constructed in such a manner that it takes an L-shape or a U-Shape. The living room is typically combined with the dining room, as well as the kitchen. The bedrooms are normally separated, and there is a patio as well as a full basement.

Obviously, this type of house is for you if you are more old-school and laid-back. You also won't find this type of home close to urban areas, so if you are a young person living and working in the city, this type of house won't be within your reach.

iii) Bungalow

A bungalow refers to a one-story house that is characterized by a sloped roof. You can always tell a bungalow apart by the dormer windows as well as verandas. Other features include:

- A roof that is low and also open.

- A small and square-shaped porch.

- A front that is compact and proportionate

Most bungalows tend to cover small square footage, even though, on occasion, you are likely to see some huge bungalows.

This design was originally adopted to provide for the needs of the working class. The particular needs of this group demanded affordability and a modern appearance.

Due to their small size, bungalows can be more affordable, especially as starter houses. This is because they tend to be cheaper and relatively easy to maintain. What's more, they tend to hold their value and appreciate over time.

Also, the fact that they are close to the ground makes them an ideal choice for the elderly and people with disabilities.

Another close benefit is that they offer more privacy than other traditional-style homes.

However, it is important to note that despite their amazing characteristics and features, bungalows are an easy target for burglars, because of their proximity to the ground. Therefore, if you make it a choice to purchase this type of home, be sure to invest in a quality security system.

iv) Mansions and McMansions

Then we have mansions and McMansions. These are houses that you can buy if you are a person of great means or exceedingly wealthy.

So what qualifies as a mansion? And what in the world is a McMansion? Let's start with the first.

A mansion is a house that covers at least 8000 square feet in floor space. So, right off the bat, these are homes that provide luxury and not needs. They are also equipped with amenities like massive gardens, tennis courts, and other high-end facilities.

A McMansion, on the other hand, are large homes that are mass-produced. They cover at least 2000 square feet in floor space. Sometimes they can be single or multi-family homes. Think of them as less bespoke versions of the more exquisite mansions.

v) Apartments

Apartments are a more popular type of housing these days.

Also known as a flat, an apartment is a self-contained type of housing that is usually part of a larger block. This is the type of housing that you are most likely to come across in areas close to big cities, especially because the land is often scarce and very expensive in areas like these.

A dwelling like this is perfect for you if you are young and work in or close to the city, and hope to do so for quite some time. It is also perfect for you if you don't want to have to worry about maintaining the exterior of your property – like lawns, driveways, etc. However, they may not be a good fit for you if you are retired and are looking for a much more laid-back and quiet lifestyle, especially because you may have to share some things and deal with next-door neighbors more than you would if you were living on a standalone property.

vi) *Condominiums*

You also have the option of purchasing condominiums.

These are units that are more or less the same as apartments. They are all part of a major residential high-rise unit. The only difference is that while most apartments are built with renting in mind, condominiums are built with the sole purpose of selling.

What's more, the occupants of condominiums collectively own the common areas such as the stairways, the corridors, the walls separating the units, the elevators, and other amenities provided like pools, tennis courts, and golf courses.

When you purchase a condominium, you end up becoming part of a Homeowners Association, and are required to contribute a monthly fee for the upkeep and maintenance of the property and its amenities.

vii) Townhouse

Another great home option is a townhouse.

A townhouse is a type of home that offers a shared ownership interest with other occupants. This is an option that is commonly found in areas where maximizing land use, due to scarcity, is essential. Think of areas like urban areas and suburbs.

This means that townhouses can have similar features to options like condos. But, it is important to note that the two are quite different. For one thing, townhouses are not a part of a high-rise building as apartments and condominiums often are. Instead, when it comes to townhouses, the units are typically arranged horizontally instead of vertically.

Since the units are adjacent to each other, there is more ownership of the walls, which is often not the case with condos. This can be advantageous because you can have more privacy, which can never be found in condos.

Also, the land under which your unit is located is also kept under your name. And since land tends to appreciate in value, you can expect townhouses to fetch a higher price in the future.

Of course, townhouses tend to be part of a homeowners association. However, the association oversees fewer details of the property, and therefore you, end up paying less in fees.

viii) Manufactured homes

Manufactured homes (also known as mobile homes), are a great option if you are low in cash and cannot afford a traditionally built home

They are also great if you are the type who keeps moving from time to time and prefer to move along with your property without incurring too much cost.

As the name suggests, this type of home is usually pre-built or assembled in a factory. So, all you need to do is purchase land and have it shipped and installed.

While this may seem like a great option for some of you, it is important to note that in many cases, lenders are not willing to offer a mortgage to finance the purchase of this type of home. This is because these homes tend to depreciate in value, and therefore lenders perceive considerable risk in co-owning them or using them as collateral.

But, if you are unconcerned with such drawbacks and can afford to finance the full purchase of this type of home, then you are good to go.

ix) Tiny home

Last but not least, you have the option of a tiny home.

If you are afraid of the large financial commitments that come with owning traditional-style homes, then you will be happy to know that owning a tiny home is an option.

These are homes that are small in space but are large enough to accommodate the needs of an individual or two. The idea is to trump the "bigger is better" philosophy that has become so popular in the world today.

The average tiny home occupies anywhere between 100 and 400 square feet. This may not be ideal for most people, but there are those in society who may be very fine with parameters like these.

Tiny homes offer you the option of living simply, with less, and with fewer financial obligations like jumbo-sized mortgages, burgeoning rent, and other types of debt, which often do affect the quality of one's life. In a debt-ridden society, these can actually be game-changer.

So which type of home is it going to be? I have provided you with the choices to pick from, but I can't make the decision for you. You will have to do that on your own. Where are you in life right now? What values are important to you? What lifestyle do you envision? These and many other questions are considerations that you will have to keep in mind as you make the ultimate choice.

8. *Effects on your job*

How will the decision to buy a home in a particular location end up affecting your job? This is something that you will seriously have to consider.

If your home ends up affecting your job negatively, that translates into a big negative. It's not something that you can afford to do.

So how do you evaluate this?

First, look at the possibility of heavy traffic. Drive to the neighborhood that you intend to belong to both during morning hours when most people go to work, and in the evening when most people come back.

What picture do you get? Do people seem to get stuck in traffic most of the time? And if so, how long does it typically take? How can this end up affecting your job performance? Will it give you more time to plan your day or wind up? Or will it make it such that you will resent going to work every day? What will your boss (or clients) think about your arrival time?

Maybe traffic isn't your problem. Perhaps the distance is. How far from your workplace is your prospective home? How much time is it likely to take you? How much fuel will it cost to take you to get there and back? Can you justify that cost?

Are you the type of person who needs a good night's sleep so that you can perform at your peak level during the day? Can you tolerate the night-time noise in the area?

Use these criteria, and perhaps more, and you might just decide that considering a different location is best.

9. *Property taxes*

Property tax is going to be part of the cost of homeownership. The local government in your place depends on it to provide social services to the community around you.

It is often charged along with your monthly mortgage payment, so it is an issue that you cannot afford to just sweep under the rug. If you become naive and choose just to ignore the matter, you could end up paying thousands of dollars more each year just to cover the cost of property taxes.

So what do you do about it? You simply find out how much it is roughly going to cost you, and you try to factor amount that in your budget. Does it fit? If it does, that's good to know.

Property tax is calculated based on the value the government places on the property in your area. The rate is a percentage of that value. Different counties will charge different rates. Often, this figure ranges between 1% and 2%, although in some counties, it goes a little beyond 2%.

Consider a home that goes for $250,000. If the rate is 1.5% in that area, it means that each year, you will have to pay $3,750 or $312.50 each month. Can you now see why property taxes can be a big issue? You want to make sure that you can afford it.

Therefore, find out from the local government or the residents in the area. And work out the numbers to see if you can take on that burden.

10. *The schools*

Do you wish to acquire a home that will uphold its value in the long-term and even withstand harsh economic conditions?

Then make sure that you purchase a home located in a good school district.

Schools have a significant impact on the value of property around them. The better the quality of a school is, the higher the demand for the property around it will be.

Countless people have indicated in surveys that they are willing to pay more – (sometimes up to 20% more) for access to homes located near a top-rated school. What's more, homes located close to high-quality schools upheld their values during the 2008 economic recession and in the years that followed it.

Why is the quality of schools such an important factor in determining the price of homes?

Well, for one thing, most people who buy homes plan on raising a family. And most of these parents want to afford their children quality education so that they can stand a great chance of success later in life. So, many people are willing to pay a premium for residential real estate located close to a top-rated school.

This is an important factor to consider, even if you have no desire to bring up a family or have kids in the near future. Just keep in mind the needs of others who may not share the same values as you, and consider purchasing a property that is close to a high-quality learning institution.

Just drive around the area and ask around. Where are the best schools in the area located? How well do they perform? How good is their curriculum? How many kids were sent to college from those institutions? Ask these and related questions, and you are likely to purchase a home with great resale value.

11. *Emergency facilities*

And what about emergency facilities? Are there any available in the area?

Life is full of surprises, both good and bad. You want to make sure that you are prepared for the bad accordingly. This means making sure that your home is located in an area with emergency facilities. So look around.

What can serve your interests during uncertain situations? For instance, imagine the case of medical emergencies. Is there a hospital nearby? How good is it? How well equipped is it?

What if there is a fire accident? Are there fire stations in the area? Do you expect them to be reliable? While you don't want your house to be too close to them, you also want to make sure that they are within reach.

And what about theft or burglary incidents? Will the police be able to respond to your case in good time? Or are they going to arrive long after the damage has been done?

All these are important considerations. Make sure you factor them in as you make your choice.

12. Fun Amenities

It is often quoted that life shouldn't be all about work. You sometimes need to take a break and smell the roses. You need to invest some time in having some fun.

So, are there amenities in the area that can cater for this need? And what value do you place on them? Which ones do you prefer to have within the community around you?

For instance, do you love playing golf? Are there golf courses within the area? Perhaps you prefer swimming, in which case you would prefer to have a swimming pool in the area. Are maybe chilling out is your style, and a park would do just fine.

Whatever your preferences are, be sure to confirm that the facilities to cater for them are present, or at least within reach.

13. Restrictions on customizations

Perhaps you are the type that loves to customize some home features. It helps to know whether you are allowed to do that.

Contrary to what you may believe, some neighborhoods and some types of properties don't allow certain customization freedoms. So, depending on your needs, you will need to inquire about these matters.

Maybe you want to paint a different color. Perhaps you want to change the design of the chimney, or you prefer to have a marble floor.

Find out whether these changes will be possible during the buying process before you commit.

14. *The age of the home*

How old should the home you expect to buy be?

Are you hoping to buy a new built that no one has ever occupied? Or are you just comfortable with purchasing older homes in more established neighborhoods?

It is important to iron out these details before a home purchase. Each decision comes with its set of benefits and drawbacks.

For instance, newer homes may come with a better and uniform design, custom features like Jacuzzis and saunas, and other trendy desirables. But, they may be more expensive, the material may be of lower quality, and the value of the home isn't time tested.

Older homes, on the other hand, may have been built with quality material that lasts. They are also more affordable. And, since they are located in more established neighborhoods, you are likely to find the landscaping to be more desirable.

On the downside, older homes may have lower resale value, they may need a lot of repairs, and the layout plus style may be out of date.

You will have to determine your taste and take your stand when it comes to this.

15. The exterior

Let's talk about the features outside the home. These can be important criteria for you to evaluate a home.

For example, do you wish to have a yard? Should it be located at the front, the back, or both? How big or small should it be? Does it have grass? Do you want it to be fenced? Or would you prefer to have an open space?

And what about a garden? How important is that to you? Do you wish to plant some crops outside? How big should it be? Does it have too many rocks? Does it slope too much?

Is there space for the kids to play? Or are they going to have to play somewhere else? Is that what you had envisioned?

What about parking? Do you plan to park outside on the driveway? Or do you prefer to have a garage? How many cars do you have, and will they all fit in the garage? What about the driveway? Can you picture yourself driving up to it and away?

Think about the view of the home. Is it important for you to have a breathtaking view? What's the architecture style – do you have any preferences? Check images of different houses with different architectural styles to start noticing if you like certain kinds of styles

You can learn more about the common architectural styles in the US from the resources below:

https://www.familyhandyman.com/list/the-top-6-most-popular-architectural-home-styles-in-the-u-s/

https://www.homestratosphere.com/home-architecture-styles/

https://www.thisoldhouse.com/21018307/american-house-styles

There is more to consider…

Is the house facing a direction that will prevent you from getting any morning sunshine? What about the pool? Will the sun be available when you plan on swimming during the afternoon? Or will it be under an annoying shade?

Are there trees outside? Do you like them? If there aren't any, are you allowed to plant your own? Or is it against the covenants in the neighborhood? Is that okay with you?

16. The interior

The interior is every bit as important as the exterior, if not more. You also want to make sure that your needs are met here as well.

What do you hope for?

There are many things to consider here. So it is up to you to come up with a list of what you wish to have. A few basics to keep in mind include the following:

- The kitchen: How big do you wish it to be, and what features should it include? Do you wish for it to have a dining area or a separate dining room? Do you want an open plan kitchen or one that is enclosed? Do you want an eat-in kitchen? Should it have an island? How big should it be? What about the countertops and cupboards– what are the deal breakers? What about built-in appliances – what comes as part of the house purchase price, and what are they made of – stainless steel or is it not so important? If it is the cooker, is it electric or gas and is either a deal-breaker?

- The bedrooms: How many do you wish to have? How big should they be? Should they provide extra storage space? Maybe you want to do some office work at home. Does your bedroom provide that? Should it have a walk-in closet, or is anything okay? What about their locations –

do you want them all located on one floor – is the location even important to you and your family? Do you want a bedroom in the ground floor, even if the house has several floors?

- Bathrooms: Generally, the rule should be, the more, the better. At minimum, consider having at least two. How many does the house you intend to live in have? Is an ensuite a MUST have or not a deal-breaker? What about the counter spaces, sinks (single or double), and the amenities in the bathroom – is a tub a big deal for you? Should it have a conventional walk-in shower and tub? How big do you want the bathroom to be? What's the location of the bathroom(s) – do you like the location?

- The living room: How big do you want it to be? Do you want a separate living and dining room? Do you want a fireplace – wood or electric?

- The basements and the attics: You need a storage place for your items. Are the attics and basements big enough to store the things you have?

- The closets: Are the realistically big enough to hold the clothes you have? And what about the storage closets where you can keep old material?

- The stairs, if any: Do you like the location and the overall layout of the house with respect to the position of the stairs? Do you like a grand entrance?

- The height of the ceilings: As they high enough to your liking?

- Extra rooms: Does the house have any other extra rooms that you can use the way you want if you want to? What are their sizes, and where are they located? For instance, if you work from home, is there a room you can convert to an office? And if you like working out, can you have a home gym or music room to put your music equipment? Do you like to have a 'man cave', recording studio, home theatre, and the likes?

Create A "Must Have" List

After going through the above items, you should have a fairly good idea of what type of home might fit your taste.

Now you are not likely to just go out there and just jump onto any opportunity that is thrown at you. You will be a more organized shopper who knows what he or she is looking for.

What you do next is create a check-list. This allows you to organize the above considerations in a way that allows you to strip out the excess information and make decisions easily and faster. After all, you don't want to carry this book around so that you can check on things as you go, do you?

I have taken the liberty to provide you with a checklist that can serve as a template. Feel free to use it or modify it to suit your needs.

Your Home-Buying Check/Wish-List

TYPE OF HOME

	NEED	BIG WANT	SMALL WANT	DON'T CARE
Single family detached				
Duplex				
Multifamily with rental unit(s)				
Condo				
Co-op apartment				
Loft / mixed use				
Single story / no stairs				

NOTES

BEDROOMS

	NEED	BIG WANT	SMALL WANT	DON'T CARE
Studio				
1				
2				
3				
4+				

NOTES

LOCATION

	NEED	BIG WANT	SMALL WANT	DON'T CARE
Urban city center				
Suburb				
Suburb with acreage				
Rural				
Water access				

NOTES

NEARBY

	NEED	BIG WANT	SMALL WANT	DON'T CARE
Employment				
Schools				
Public transportation				
Airport				
Bike paths				
Shops and restaurants				
Cultural & arts opportunities				
Community center				
Recreation, parks, playgrounds				

NOTES

PARKING

	NEED	BIG WANT	SMALL WANT	DON'T CARE
Garage				
Carport				
Driveway / off-street				

NOTES

BATHROOMS

	NEED	BIG WANT	SMALL WANT	DON'T CARE
1				
2				
2.5-3				
4+				

NOTES

ROOM FEATURES

	NEED	BIG WANT	SMALL WANT	DON'T CARE
Open plan				
Great room				
Formal livingroom				
Formal dining room				
Eat-in kitchen				
Master suite with bath				
Walk-in closets				
Home office				
Attic				
Finished basement				
Laundry room				
Screened porch				

NOTES

KITCHEN

	NEED	BIG WANT	SMALL WANT	DON'T CARE
Eat-in				
Breakfast bar				
Island				
New appliances				
Stone countertops				
New / remodeled cabinetry				
Pantry				

NOTES

FLOORING

	NEED	BIG WANT	SMALL WANT	DON'T CARE
Hardwood				
Manufactured wood				
Cork or bamboo				
Laminate				
Wall-to-wall carpet				
Tile				
Stone				

NOTES

EXTERIOR

	NEED	BIG WANT	SMALL WANT	DON'T CARE
Brick				
Wood				
Shingle				
Stone				
Stucco				
Low maintenance				

NOTES

HEATING / COOLING

	NEED	BIG WANT	SMALL WANT	DON'T CARE
Electric				
Natural gas / propane				
Radiant heat				
Central Air				
Fireplace				
Fireplace with insert				
Wood or pellet stove				

NOTES

ENERGY EFFICIENCY

	NEED	BIG WANT	SMALL WANT	DON'T CARE
Insulation and air sealing				
Solar panels				
Solar ready				
Tankless water heater				
Heat-pump water heater				
Dual- or triple-pane windows				
Low-flow toilets				
Energy Star appliances				
Programmable thermostats				

NOTES

OUTDOOR SPACE		NEED	BIG WANT	SMALL WANT	DON'T CARE
	Yard				
	Fenced yard				
	Trees / landscaping / gardens				
	Automatic sprinklers				
	Deck				
	Patio				
	Covered porch				
	Courtyard				
	Pool				
	Outbuildings:				

NOTES

UNIVERSAL DESIGN FEATURES		NEED	BIG WANT	SMALL WANT	DON'T CARE
	Extra-wide doorways				
	Ramp				
	Elevator				
	Grab bars				
	Accessible kitchen				
	Walk-in tub / shower				

NOTES

Images courtesy of *frameworkhomeownership.org*

You can use this checklist to narrow down your search.

There are also other checklists from these resource:

https://www.weichert.com/guides/checklist/home-buying-wishlist/

Of course, it is virtually impossible to find a home that meets your exact needs. The more flexible you can be, the more choices you will have. Therefore, a checklist like this is not meant to box you in an all-or-nothing situation.

The key is to establish acceptable parameters. You have to ask yourself, "What is the least that I can expect from a home that I want to buy based on the checklist or wishlist above?" Once you can answer that question well, finding a home will be a whole lot easier.

In the next section, we will look at financing. We will explore the available options on the market, including tips on how to evaluate lenders. See you there.

Securing Financing

If you are like most people, you probably realize that you will need financial assistance to purchase your dream home. Few people have the means to purchase their homes in cash.

The fact is, homes are very expensive. You will be looking at figures that go well beyond $100,000 for fairly small-sized traditional homes in many locations. Homes with an aesthetic appeal are even pricier. And the more urbanized the place is, the more money you can expect to pay for less square footage and amenities!

Since most people do not have sizeable fortunes stashed away for purposes of buying a home, this leaves you with the option of having to do business with lenders.

Doing business with lenders can be a tricky affair. You will be dealing with people that are in the game to make money. People who are looking after their own best interests. People who are interested in taking home a sizeable check.

In the light of this knowledge, you will need to show up at the chessboard armed with sufficient knowledge about the kind of game you are playing, and the various options that you have because knowledge is your best weapon.

So in this chapter, we will strip down the subject of financing the purchase of your home down to its bones. You will no longer feel clueless about which decision is best for you.

We'll start from the beginning

What Is A Mortgage?

A mortgage is simply a type of loan that is extended to someone who intends to fund the purchase of a home.

Lending is a very simple concept; you are given money by a certain party - That party is interested in getting their money back along with a nice profit on top of it. That profit is called interest.

But you already know this. You've probably borrowed several times in your life by now. A mortgage is no different. You will be required to pay for a portion of the total cost of your home; then, you borrow to fund the rest of the purchase. After that, you will need to start making monthly payments meant to service your debt.

Perhaps the biggest difference you will note is that mortgages charge less interest when compared to other types of credit. For instance, credit cards can charge high interest that can go as high as 20%+ APR. Mortgages cost a lot less. You can easily find a mortgage that charges 6% give or take, in interest.

So, if you are careful, mortgages may not land you into much trouble, provided you borrow what you can afford.

It is important to note that, when you take a mortgage, you end up co-owning the home with your lender. Your lender does this to protect its financial interests.

If for some reason, you ever run into trouble and can no longer pay your mortgage, your lender will mitigate its risk by selling the house on the market to recoup the original investment. This type of action is known as a foreclosure.

So, now that you are familiar with what a mortgage is and how it works let's move up a little and talk about…

The Different Types of Mortgages

What types of mortgage options do you have?

They are quite a number. However, it helps to know that they all fall into two basic categories. Those categories are:

i)   Fixed-rate mortgages

This type of mortgage is exactly what its name refers to; the interest rate on this type of mortgage is specific throughout the life of the loan. If you take out a loan at 6% interest, you will keep paying that interest to the day when you finish your entire mortgage payment.

Fixed-rate mortgages are generally a good idea, and I highly recommend them, especially if you are an unsophisticated person. They will make your life a whole lot easier.

Why do I say this?

Simple; because you are required to pay a specific amount each month.

Let me give you an example to illustrate this:

Let's say that you took out a 15-year mortgage and got the bank to agree to finance $150,000 of the purchase price at 6.5% interest. This means that each month, you will be required to pay $1,306.

This is good because it is predictable. You can essentially budget for this amount and include it in your monthly plans.

Nevertheless, there is a catch. There are never free lunches when it comes to borrowing on mortgages.

The basic catch is, interest rates on fixed-rate mortgages are always higher than those on adjustable-rate mortgages. But this is with good reason. You see, the lender is taking on more risk by providing you with a stable monthly payment. If interest rates rise, then they will be stuck in a bad situation that causes them to lose money with your loan. Your lender hopes to offset the risk of this situation by charging more interest.

Also, a fixed-rate mortgage also means that you cannot easily take advantage of a rising economy. Keep in mind that interest rates always fluctuate depending on market conditions. When the economy is booming, they are low, and when the economy is on the rocks, they are very high.

If your interest rate is fixed and the economy ends up performing better than expected during the lifetime of your loan, you won't take advantage of the situation.

Of course, you can always fix this issue by doing what is called refinancing. This is where you take a new mortgage on your home that has better terms that reflect the current market conditions. But, such deals take time and money.

Nevertheless, I tend to think that fixed-rate mortgages carry less risk.

ii) Adjustable-rate mortgages

On the other end of the spectrum, you have what are known as adjustable-rate mortgages (ARMs).

These are simply the opposite of fixed-rate mortgages. These are mortgages that have an interest rate that adjusts according to the market conditions. These changes can be in your favor or against you.

Unlike their counterparts, you can never establish predictability with these types of mortgages. Your monthly payments can go up or down, depending on the economic situation. This makes it a lot harder to plan your future payments accordingly, and with ease.

Why do people still take these types of mortgages?

Well, the first reason has to do with how these mortgages are structured and marketed. ARMs are usually marketed to the public with special lower beginner rates that make them sound more of a better deal than they actually are. These rates are called *teaser rates*.

You will find that most marketers are keen on emphasizing the teaser rate, more than anything else. The goal is to make you feel that purchasing an expensive home is well within your means.

What most people who are attracted to the low teaser rates aren't usually aware of is that these rates usually adjust later on. And that adjustment is usually upwards. So, essentially, you begin with small, manageable payments that eventually go up in a few months or so. If you are not prepared, the sudden surge in payments can end up eating you alive.

The danger of Adjustable Rate Mortgages

It is easy to see why these mortgages can be dangerous, mainly because they were the hallmark of the 2008 economic crisis. What basically happened is that bankers and other mortgage lenders suddenly increased their appetite for risk in the pursuit of big profits, without observing well-established business principles.

At the same time, most people ignored logical reason and fell into the trap of believing that owning a home was well within their means (even though it wasn't for most of them). The result was that both parties lost big time and plunged the world into a recession.

It happened like this: In the earlier years preceding 2008, the economy was booming, and the lending business was doing better than it had for decades. Almost anybody who touched a mortgage made money in those days. It almost felt like a no-risk situation.

The good times fooled many into believing that the situation was normal and that it would continue indefinitely. People just became euphoric.

The euphoria led many into believing that they were actually smarter than they really were. Many people began overextending themselves—lenders, in particular, engaged in very risky activity.

Lenders began creating mortgage products meant for "risky borrowers" or "sub-prime borrowers" as they are called in the financial world. Subprime borrowers are people whose credit score is really poor.

Most have no income and no jobs. Basically, subprime borrowers are in a financial hole. In those days, some didn't even have identification documents. It's almost impossible to fathom how such borrowers could have credit extended to them, but greed was so much that common sense didn't prevail in those glory days.

As former Merrill Lynch CEO, John Thain, recalls, "The loans were dubbed **NINJA** loans in the financial circles. Meaning **No Income No Job**."

The risk of default is with such borrowers is almost certain. Yet, with the booming economy, it was assumed that cutting deals with such borrowers was actually safe- subprime borrowers were offered deals such as **"no money down"** – meaning no deposit necessary (hence the name **interest-only mortgages**). The borrower simply assumed the largest part of the risk.

It was as toxic as loan products get, but in the short term, everything just seemed to work out just fine. The subprime borrowers were managing the teaser rate payments, and so it was assumed that they could manage later payments – an erroneous assumption.

So, with these mortgages performing well on books, they were even sold off to other big banks on Wall Street, so that lenders could free up cash to do more business – a common practice in financial circles. The Wall Street banks later turned around and securitized these toxic loans, so that they could be sold to the public as investable products.

So, these toxic products became tradable in the interbank markets, much in the same way stocks and bonds are bought and sold. Massive personal and corporate portfolios were built around these *"mortgage-backed securities."*

Then reality set in. After some time, the teaser rate periods on these loans were over, and the rates adjusted. Many of these adjustments were large and unexpected. In some instances, monthly mortgage payments went up as much as four or even five times.

Since most borrowers were people of small means, they couldn't manage these payments. Large numbers of people were stuck in houses with mortgage payments that they couldn't afford. And as is customary, when mortgages failed to perform, foreclosures followed.

Keep in mind that some of these homes were sold on **"no money down"** terms. So homeowners found it easier to walk away from their homes during foreclosure, leaving the lenders holding the bag.

And since these non-performing loans had been bought by other investors on Wall Street and around the world, the result was that these investments began failing. Banks that had bought these risky securities lost money, and many were forced to close down. Also, private investors lost money, and the world fell into an economic recession.

And that, in a nutshell, is the danger associated with Adjustable Rate Mortgages. When abused, the results can be devastating.

Nevertheless, there are special instances when taking on an Adjustable Rate Mortgage can be desirable. Also, the government, banks, and lending institutions have grown wiser about ARMs, and how they can be used, in order to prevent catastrophes. We'll talk more about how you can use them later on in this chapter.

For now, let's talk about other types of mortgages that you need to know of.

iii) Hybrid mortgages

Hybrid mortgages are a special type of mortgage.

They are the result of the constant innovation that takes place in the world of finance.

A hybrid mortgage is special because it incorporates features of both a fixed-rate mortgage as well as those of an adjustable one.

Here's what I mean: with a hybrid mortgage, you are allowed to pay a fixed rate for a certain amount of time. Afterward, the loan takes on the nature of an adjustable-rate mortgage.

This type of loan has been created, taking into consideration those home buyers that are not interested in staying in one home for a very long time. If this describes you, then you will find this mortgage product useful.

This loan can be useful if you are looking to purchase a home in a rising market, but hope to leave it soon and would like to have some predictability in housing payments during that time.

You see, hybrid mortgages can have five, six, seven, even ten years, requiring a fixed-rate payment. After that period, the rate becomes adjustable. This is well within reason, of course, because lenders know that many first-time homebuyers never stay in the same house for more than seven years.

If the market is performing well, you can easily sell the house and pass on the mortgage to someone else.

iv) Balloon mortgages

Lastly, there is what is known as a balloon mortgage, otherwise known as a bullet loan.

It functions a lot like a hybrid mortgage. It starts as a fixed-rate mortgage and stays that way for some time, say 7 years or so. Then after the fixed-rate period is over, the mortgage, instead of switching to an adjustable-rate period, simply matures!

Yes, that's right. The mortgage matures – you are required to pay the full amount then and there.

It is for this reason that the loan is called a balloon mortgage. It is a name that ties to some sort of joke in the financial world... the loan literally **blows up** in your face at maturity.

It is nothing different from the name *bullet loan*. Experts in finance describe the feeling that the borrower gets when the loan matures, especially if interest rates happen to be high at the time of maturity to be almost the same as that of getting hit by a bullet.

Obviously, this is a risky loan product, and I see no reason why you should ever consider it. The exception, of course, is if you are absolutely certain that you can come up with a substantial amount of money at maturity to pay off the full loan.

When should you consider an adjustable-rate loan?

So, under what circumstances should you consider taking an ARM? After all, they are not all bad news. As I mentioned before, changes have taken place, which has made these mortgages a lot safer than they used to be.

One positive aspect to consider is that ARMs come with much lower interest rates when compared with fixed-rate mortgages. Your lender is willing to cut you some slack for assuming the risk of fluctuating interest rates. Lenders don't extend that level of professional courtesy to borrowers who try to be as most risk aversive as they possibly can.

Also, keep in mind that the economy may, in fact, improve. You can usually do some kind of analysis that may attempt to predict the future prospects of the economy. Enlightened real estate brokers and financial analysts can help you with this task.

Nobody can predict accurately where the economy will be in the next 15 or 30 years, any more than anyone can foretell the future. But, economic indicators and data analysis can provide reliable clues that can aid your decision-making process and mitigate risk.

These are the same procedures that lenders use when they try to devise methods of minimizing risk in their business. If they can do it without placing themselves in a precarious situation, so can you. But, you must be willing to go through the trouble to get access to that kind of information, even pay for it if you have to.

Another reason why ARMs have become less risky is that they have caps. Caps are there to keep payable interest from getting too high or too low. This is meant to prevent a scenario whereby a mortgage becomes too expensive or to cheap.

Therefore, you will find that some mortgages have a cap that keeps them from adjusting more or less than 2% annually or 6% over the lifetime of the loan.

These are some of the reasons why ARMs are still viable if you are willing to take some risk.

That said, here are the instances under which ARMs can be considered.

1) You have a solid budget that shows that you can cover the highest expected mortgage payment should interest rates move against you during the life of the loan, while still allowing you to achieve important financial goals like saving for retirement or your children's education. Your lender should reveal to you the highest mortgage payment you can be expected to make.

2) You have a fully-funded emergency fund that covers at least 6 months' worth of living costs. This is important

because you may tap into it to cover unexpected mortgage payment hikes.

3) You are almost certain that you have a stable job, and that your income prospects are looking very good for the foreseeable future, and that you won't struggle. If you are a self-employed business owner, you may never be too sure about this unless your business is a pretty established brand.

4) If you have a family and expect more kids in the future, you have calculated and are comfortable with the rise in the cost of living that comes with the arrival of those children.

5) You have established that you are very stable psychologically and that changes in mortgage payments won't push you to the edge causing significant stress or possibly bringing about illnesses.

Stated simply, for you to even consider ARMs, you must be in a very stable financial and psychological position. Few people are in such a position, and that is why I generally do not recommend them. They can turn your life around for the worst.

Sure, given the characteristics of ARMS, you might be able to save a lot of money in the long run if the odds move in your favor. But that comes at a price that most people are not willing to pay.

You just have to work out the most important thing to you. If peace of mind is more important than saving money, then fixed-rate mortgages may be a better fit. After all, you could devise other ways to earn more money for yourself.

Now let's get to talking about fees charged by mortgage lenders, because they are part of the overall cost of buying a home, and should never be ignored.

Fees Charged By Mortgage Lenders

The initial deposit on the purchase price of the home isn't the only amount of money that your lender will require you to foot in during the closing of the deal on your home.

There are other fees involved that you need to be aware of. Knowing that they exist will prevent surprises at the time of closing. These surprises may drain you of all money and possibly push you into debt. Here they are:

1. Points

The first type of fee that you can expect to get charged by a lender is known as a point.

A point is a one-time fee that a lender charges you as compensation for the work done in processing your mortgage as well as approving it.

This fee is always expressed as a percentage of the total loan amount. Think of a mortgage loan that amounts to $200,000. If the lender quotes that the point on loan is 2%, it means that you will have to pay $4,000 at the time of closing the home deal.

Now, you must note that paying points always means that the lender will reduce your interest rate burden. That is to say, that a loan that requires you to pay points will be a lot cheaper than a loan that doesn't.

For instance, your lender may offer to lend you $200K loan at 6% interest rate and 1% in points. At the same time, they may provide a loan for an equivalent amount at 7% interest with no points.

So, you may be wondering whether paying the points is better than not. Well, the fact of the matter is that it depends on how long you intend to keep the loan. If you intend to pay the loan in as little time as possible, then paying the point is usually not worth it.

But, if you intend to keep paying the loan over a long time (say 30 years), you could really use the interest rate discount. This is because a small interest differential can make a big difference over many years.

Let me illustrate the point I am trying to make here. How much will you end up saving, if you get your interest rate reduced by 1%? Let's take the example of a loan amount of 200K at 6.5% and 1% in points versus one that goes for 7%. We'll assume that both loans last 30 years.

At the end of the 30 years, you will have paid a total of $255,088 on the first loan versus $279,017. That's a difference of $23,929. Factor in the $2,000 that you will need to pay at closing and you will have saved yourself a full **$21,929**, simply by accepting a loan that requires you to pay a 1% point. That is not loose change.

Can you see why sometimes it makes a lot of sense to just pay up the point? If you have a loan that lasts long, you can save yourself tens of thousands of dollars down the road.

What's more, points paid on a mortgage application are usually tax-deductible. So that's an added advantage. You might want to consult with your CPA on this one.

2. *Appraisal Fee*

The next type of fee that you ought to be aware of is the appraisal fee.

This fee goes to the appraiser approved by the lender to inspect the property you hope to buy. The role of the appraiser is to ascertain the market value of the property that you wish to purchase.

This information is critical because it helps the lender determine the true value of the home and how much they are willing to extend in credit. You see, the lender doesn't care that you agreed to pay a price that is well above market value.

The lender only wants to protect their own financial interest so that in the case that the loan goes bad and they have to foreclose on the home, they don't end up in more trouble than envisioned.

So, if you were applying for a $250K loan, and the report from the appraiser reveals that the home is worth only $200k, then you will have to come up with the remaining $50k because the lender won't be taking responsibility for that.

3. Credit report fees

At this point, you already know that a lender will need to do a background check on your creditworthiness before they can agree to do business with you.

This means that the lender will have to query for your credit reports from relevant authorities so that they can go over your credit history and look at your bill payment patterns, how much you owe to different parties, whether you always pay in time, and so on.

Getting access to these credit reports doesn't come free. Therefore, the cost of getting access to these documents is going to be passed over to you.

Now, you probably understand the value of putting your finances in order before you decide to approach a lender. If your financial situation is poor and you head out to inquire about loans from a lender, you will be wasting both time and money because your application may be rejected, and the lender won't refund you the cost involved in uncovering this fact.

4. Application processing fee

The application processing fee is a fee that the lender charges you for the trouble involved in checking out your credit history and submitting your loan application for approval.

Lenders charge this fee, as a way for compensating themselves for the time and effort spent, should your loan fail to materialize.

A few lenders are willing to refund this amount if your loan gets processed and approved.

Now that you are aware of the different fees that you may be charged, what do you do now? One simple thing you could do is simply ask your lender to provide you with an itemized list of the different fees involved. Once you have this list, you can simply start planning ahead of time to come up with the amount required.

One more thing: you may come across lenders who claim to charge no fees. Don't buy into it. Remember, there are no free lunches in this business. What usually happens is that these fees are charged up to other costs involved in the loan, such as points or interest.

Now let us look at areas where you can shop for loans and how you can select the right lender to work with.

How To Shop For And Select A Mortgage Product

So how do you go about finding and securing a mortgage that is right for you? After all, there are countless options out there. Here are some places to consider.

1. *Online*

This is perhaps the greatest gift to all humanity living in the information era. Information on almost anything is readily available at the click of a button.

Provided you own a computer, possess a few basic skills, and have subscribed to a reliable internet connection, you can research mortgage lenders and their rates from the comfort of your couch at home.

There are websites on the web that do a good job of presenting you with a great deal of information about lenders on the mortgage market. All you have to do is head up to them and perform a search.

You just have to know what you are looking for, and the search will be a lot easier. Some websites will require you to provide your personal information, though. Obviously, this is done to provide leads to sellers of mortgage products. You can expect to be contacted with offers if you use these sites. It is up to you to decide whether you prefer using the sites at all.

So, I have made it my business to compile a small list of websites that I have found to be useful in helping locate different lenders and their rates; your research may turn up a longer list.

Perhaps some of these websites will no longer be in existence by the time you read this book. But, I firmly believe quite a number will be around for the long haul and that this list will serve as an excellent starting point for your research.

Here it is:

Bankrate: https://www.bankrate.com/mortgages/mortgage-rates/

Money Supermarket: https://www.moneysupermarket.com/mortgages/rates-table/first-time-buyer/

Nerdwallet: https://www.nerdwallet.com/mortgages/mortgage-rates

Smartasset: https://smartasset.com/mortgage/mortgage-rates

Realtor.com: https://www.realtor.com/mortgage/rates/

Quicken Loans: https://www.quickenloans.com/l/progpi

Zillow: https://www.zillow.com/mortgage-rates/#/location

C – Loans: https://www.c-loans.com/

Comparethemarket: https://www.comparethemarket.com/mortgages/

HSH: https://www.hsh.com/

It is important to note that each of these websites has databases that list only a limited number of lenders. Therefore, for a more comprehensive research process, make sure to check more than just one website.

2. Newspapers

Another good place to research possible lenders for your mortgage is in newspapers.

Most popular newspapers contain ads and real estate sections that publish lists of lenders, along with their rates. This list can provide additional options to the list of lenders that you may have already compiled from your online research.

You do need to be careful about one thing though. Newspapers frequently publish outdated information on interest rates. And since the information is not updatable, the rates you see in the newspaper may not be the rates that the lender is currently offering. Make a point of inquiring for clarification before you make major assumptions.

3. Mortgage brokers

You can also find great deals by consulting mortgage brokers.

In case you do not know, mortgage brokers are simply middlemen who help home buyers get through the process of finding a suitable mortgage deal and dealing with the necessary paperwork to completion. They get paid a percentage of the amount closed on a mortgage deal.

Since mortgage brokers have been involved in countless deals in the past, they are often good sources of information on great deals.

What's more, a mortgage broker can help you find lenders who can finance your home purchase, especially in instances where your past credit history has left few lenders willing to give you money.

Also, a mortgage broker can help you find lenders who are willing to finance unusual purchases like condos and expensive mansions. Properties like these are usually not the bread and butter of most lenders, and you may hit a roadblock on your quest in trying to find one who is willing. An experienced mortgage broker can help straighten things out in this department.

So, if you are having problems with finding time to carry out your research or would like to expand the parameters and find out whether other great options exist, then mortgage brokers are a nice bunch of people to consult.

4. Real estate brokers

Real estate brokers are also great consultants on mortgage information.

Unlike mortgage brokers, real estate brokers are involved in the process of helping buyers and sellers of property find each other. There are real estate brokers who represent sellers, and there are those who represent buyers. Some represent both sides.

An experienced real estate broker has contacts with reputable lenders and can be a great time-saver in the process of research. A good real estate agent can easily point out which lenders are likely to close on deals and those that often back out during critical moments, often frustrating the buyers. He or she has seen it all.

If you wish to avoid ugly inconveniences, then consulting a top-gun real estate agent can prove to be worthwhile. Of course, you will have to pay premium fees to work with them, but I can assure you that, in many instances, they are worth it. We will talk about how you can select a good real estate agent later. For now, just understand that they can provide valuable research data on mortgages.

Now that you have an idea of how you can go about shopping for, mortgages let's move up and talk about how you can qualify or disqualify lenders that you can work with.

How To Choose A Lender To Work With

How do you know which lender is good for you? You know...one that will not put their interests above everything else?

It's true; lenders are in the business to make money. But you don't want to work with someone who is too hell-bent on making money, to the point of doing everything under the sun so that their objective is realized.

You want to work with someone who understands that you are a human being, and who will treat you accordingly.

So how do you go about assessing a lender who is likely to take care of your interests as well? There are several points you can employ. Here are some good ones.

1. A lender who is straightforward

Dealing with mortgages can be a mighty headache. You have all these complicated terms like points, amortization, index, markup, and so on. And since you are not a real estate professional, all these details can make your head spin.

Now, when choosing a lender to work with, you want someone who will make your life easier, not harder. You want him or her to explain all their products and terms in language that the average person can understand.

That is precisely what professional lenders ought to do. You don't want a lender who will try to impress you with doubletalk and expensive language filled with jargon only a banker would love.

If you find a lender who is keen on confusing you with complicated terms, then you should be looking to take your business elsewhere. Such a lender may have a hidden agenda and may not look out for your best interests in the future. At the very least, you can expect unwanted surprises in the future for not understanding what he or she was trying to explain.

Remember, this is your hard-earned money you will be putting on the line. You deserve to understand every detail involved in what can count as the most important financial decision of your life. The moment you find a lender who is trying to blur things with expensive talk, run away as fast you possibly can.

2. *A lender who approves locally*

You also want a lender who makes important decisions, such as loan approval locally.

Some lenders make a point of overcomplicating the process by having to send your loan application to an out-of-town office in some major city or something. This can be a sign that you shouldn't be working with that lender.

Why?

Because the moment your application goes to another office, you stop being perceived as a person. You become a loan number, a statistic to work with. There is no room for negotiations or explaining yourself and your situation.

The last thing you want is your lender treating you like some inanimate object. The best lenders approve deals at the local office. This way, they can call you at any time to explain and clarify certain pressing problems and even negotiate loan terms. You may even want to tag along your real estate agent to advise you accordingly during this process.

Lenders who approve loans elsewhere are likely to be the type that frustrates you by backing out on a deal at the last minute simply because the property doesn't meet some obscure company policy or something. Get a lender who makes decisions locally, and you'll have an easier time.

How do you find out whether a lender meets this requirement? Simple. Just ask. Let it be one of the questions you ask before you get into discussing important aspects of the loan you are seeking.

3. A lender who has extensive local market knowledge

You want a lender who knows the local real estate market well and who will immediately understand what you are looking for right from the start.

Such a lender has been around for quite some time and works with local professionals.

For instance, you don't want a lender who will recommend an appraiser who isn't a local resident and that is familiar with local property prices, and who hasn't participated in a large number of closed deals.

You can simply ask around whether the lender fits this requirement. You can learn a lot from the locals. Experienced real estate agents can also provide this information.

4. A lender who is willing to negotiate

The estate business is full of negotiations.

You can negotiate for lower rates from real estate agents and mortgage brokers. You can also negotiate property prices with sellers of homes. The same goes for rates and terms from lenders.

You want a lender who is open to negotiation. You see, lending is a remarkably competitive business. In most cases, you will find several lenders who provide lower rates and more favorable terms when compared to others.

You want a lender who is well aware that there are many other options out there that you could consider. Such a lender should not try to box you in. At the very least, they should appreciate the research that you have conducted and be willing to match the rates of those competitors you have uncovered.

If a lender insists on not knocking down the rates they are offering, try, and find out why. If there is nothing better that he or she is bringing to the table, then you will definitely want to take your business elsewhere.

5. A lender who keeps their word

Last but not least, the lender you choose to work with must have integrity. They must have a reputation of keeping their word.

As I've said before, some lenders may back out at the last minute for relatively insignificant reasons. Such a lender may cost you a property that you may have invested a great deal of time, effort, and emotions on.

Just ask an enlightened real estate agent who has participated in many deals in the area whether your chosen lender has a history of disappointing clients during critical moments.

If you follow these simple guidelines, you will hardly select a lender who will frustrate you in the years to come. Remember, this is the lender who will stick with you for as much as 30 years or so. So it pays to go through the trouble to evaluate them.

Evaluating a lender based on rates alone isn't enough. It's sometimes better to pay more for a reputable lender who will save you headaches down the road.

Now, let's move on and talk about how you can evaluate the actual mortgage products that you will be considering.

How To Evaluate Mortgage Products

Let's now talk about how you get to choose from a list of mortgage products. How do you select the right product?

We'll first talk about how you can select from a list of fixed-rate mortgages. Later on, we can talk about how you can choose the right adjustable-rate mortgage.

i) *Selecting a fixed-rate mortgage*

Fixed-rate mortgages are the easiest to select. This is because they involve much fewer details when compared to adjustable-rate mortgages. Thus, you will have an easier time with these ones.

So, the first thing you need to keep in mind is that you will be looking for the lowest rate. That isn't difficult at all, is it? From the list that you may have in your hands, whether it is one from a broker or one that you have created yourself, just look for the lender that has the lowest rate in it.

But the search doesn't stop there. Find out what the fees and closing costs will end up costing you. For instance, fixed-rate mortgages are likely to have points. You have to factor that in as well.

So how do you determine how much a fixed-rate mortgage is likely to cost you in total, with fees factored in? Simple. Just look at the APR.

Mortgage lenders will always advertise two figures, the interest rate, and the APR. The interest rate is what you will pay year after year to compensate the lender for lending you their money. The APR, on the other hand, is a percentage that factors in other expenses associated with taking out the loan.

Therefore, an APR is a much better reflection of what the loan will end up costing you. So, you not only want to check out the interest, you want to look at the APR as well. The one with the lowest interest rate, as well as APR is your best pick.

ii) Selecting an adjustable-rate mortgage

What if you have made up your mind, that despite the wisdom contained in this book, that adjustable-rate mortgages are a much better fit for you? Well, you will have to know how to evaluate those as well.

Now, when it comes to adjustable-rate mortgages, it helps to know a little bit more. You need to know about the index, as well as the margin.

You've never heard of these terms before, so let's talk about what they mean for a moment.

What is an index?

An index is a reference point for a mortgage lender as to what the current interest rates are. An index helps the mortgage lender calculate how much it costs them to borrow the money that they later lend to you.

If the index goes up, then that is a reflection that interest rates have gone up and that borrowing is actually costing the lender more. If it goes down, then that is a sign that interest rates have gone down too, and that money is much cheaper.

Mortgage products from different lenders can be based on various indexes. It's all a matter of preference. Some popular indexes used by lenders are:

- Treasury bills
- Certificates of deposit
- The 11th District Cost of Funds Index (COFI)
- The London Interbank Offered Rate Index (LIBOR)

So, if the interest rate on a 6 month Treasury bill is 5%, a lender that relies on this index will use that figure to determine how much it costs them to borrow money.

What is margin?

What about margin (otherwise known as markup)?

Margin is simply the profit that the lender hopes to make on loan. This number is usually added to the index to establish the overall interest rate on loan.

So, for instance, if the margin on a loan product is 2.5% and it is pegged to a 6-month Treasury bill interest rate of 5%, then the overall interest rate on loan is 7.5%.

So, what do you with this knowledge? Use it to compare loans against each other.

The first thing you want to do is make sure that you compare one ARM product against another, only if they are pegged to the same index. Once you have ascertained that this is the case, then check to see which one has the lowest margin.

You do this because different indexes will have different rates and will also fluctuate differently. So it makes no sense to treat them equally.

You also want to make sure you check the APR. This gives you an estimate of how much the loan will end up costing you in fees. Of course, all factors being constant, the one with the lower APR is the better one.

Another factor you want to check out is the frequency of adjustment. Generally, the rule here is that the higher the frequency of adjustment, the higher the risk you end up bearing. Some loans will adjust every month, others every six months, and others every year.

I recommend that you only pick the ones that either adjust every 6 or 12 months. Anything below that rough threshold is likely to put you in a precarious position.

Lastly, you want to check the rate caps. The cap restricts the amount of interest rate fluctuation either up or down, thus providing some sort of protection for both the lender and the borrower.

First, I recommend that you stay away from loans that have no caps. Those are way too risky. Then, select only those that have a maximum cap of 2% on an annual basis and 6% over the life of the loan.

Obviously, as you can see, ARMs require you to be a little more sophisticated, both in terms of your risk profile as well as the knowledge and the amount of work you are willing to do. Fixed-rate mortgages are more of a walk in the park. You have to establish what type of person you are and the level of trouble you are willing to accept.

That said, now you have a good idea of how you can select an appropriate product if presented with a list.

Other Things To Consider

Before we close the curtain on the topic of mortgages, there are some things you need to know. It helps to know about them because you can plan accordingly.

1. Government-insured loans

The government is strongly behind the idea that most Americans be able to afford a home. And it shows that commitment by insuring mortgages for members of society who meet certain eligibility requirements.

By insuring, the government guaranteed to step in and cover the loan if you happen to default on the loan.

So, it helps to know about these loans, their minimum requirements, and whether the lender you are considering offers them. Depending on your situation, taking these mortgages may be a good idea.

These include:

i) *VA loans*

VA stands for Veterans Affairs. The U.S Department of Veterans Affairs insures VA loans. They are afforded to members of the public who are veterans, surviving spouses of veterans, the military personnel who are on active duty, as well as reservists.

These loans are unique because you don't need to make any down payment, acquire private mortgage insurance, or have a perfect credit score.

So, if you belong to that category of people who are eligible for this loan, then you will be happy to discover that you have such a unique opportunity. However, keep in mind that your credit score has to be at least at 580 *(refer to the first chapter for information on this)*.

ii) *FHA loans*

FHA stands for Federal Housing Administration. The Federal Housing Administration guarantees these loans. The thing about these loans is that they are not just offered by any lender; you will only get them from lenders approved by the FHA.

So who qualifies for a FHA loan?

First of all, these loans are offered while keeping first-time homebuyers who are looking to purchase a primary residence in mind - that is, people like you. Second, these loans are afforded to low-to-medium income earners.

So what is the primary benefit of this type of loan?

Well, unlike conventional loans, you do not have to come up with a huge down-payment of 10%, 20%, or perhaps more. The minimum down-payment required with this type of loan is only 3.5%.

Now, despite this, you will need to acquire and pay for mortgage insurance. We will talk about mortgage insurance in a moment.

It is worth keeping in mind that, just like the VA loan, this type of mortgage requires that you have a minimum credit score of 580.

iii) USDA

This is a loan that is insured by the US Department of Agriculture.

It is aimed at those who want to purchase homes in rural areas that aren't densely populated. There are certain dimensions provided by the USDA that qualifies a neighborhood as being rural.

The beauty of this loan is that you won't have to place any down-payment. You will, however, need to pay what is known as a guarantee fee instead. Of course, this figure is much lower than a typical down-payment. But, a mortgage insurance is very much a requirement.

The minimum credit score you will need to have to qualify for this loan is a bit higher, at 620.

So, if you still have the desire to buy a home, but don't qualify for a conventional loan either because you can't afford a sizeable down-payment, or have issues with your credit, then you might want to seek lenders who offer these type of loans.

iv) Good neighbor next door

This program is offered by the U.S Department of Housing and Urban Development (or HUD).

It is a unique program in that it allows qualified participants to acquire a home for a steep discount of up to 50%. Just think about that.

These homes are located in areas that the HUD designates as "revitalized areas." Revitalized areas are areas characterized by several things, among them including:

- The number of foreclosures on homes backed by FHA-insured mortgages
- The ownership rate of homes in the area
- The average household income

Typically, when the houses under this program come onto the market, they are offered for sale for a maximum period of seven days. During this time, you can purchase the program at a discounted price. But, if it turns out that there are many contestants to the properties, a random lottery will be employed to select winners who get the homes.

Now, for you to take advantage of this program, you must be a first-time homebuyer who is a first responder or a trainer. You do qualify for the program if you are in any of these professions:

- An emergency medical technician
- A teacher for grades pre-K to 12

- A firefighter

- A law enforcement officer

It is important to note that this home will need to be your primary residence for at least 3 years.

v) *Fannie Mae's HomePath Ready Buyer Program*

This is another unique program offered by Fannie Mae.

It is unique in that it allows you to put up only 3% down on a property that has been designated as a HomePath property (you can locate such properties on sale by browsing the HomePath website).

Furthermore, you are allowed up to 3% to take care of closing costs, provided you agree to take the course offered by Fannie Mae. If you end up going through with the sale, you also get a refund on the course fee. This truly a bargain.

The course covers a few basic but truly important topics such as:

- How you can determine the right home for you

- Calculating how much house you can afford

- How you can stay away from common issues

If you are purchasing the home as a couple, or with some other party, then only one of you will be required to take the course.

Now, for you to qualify for such a program, you have to meet the following requirements:

- You must be classified as a first-time homebuyer
- You must move and make the house a primary residence within 60 days after the deal is closed
- The property you intend to buy must be a HomePath property.

You are required to have an agent to help you with the negotiation process, and for you to qualify for the closing cost assistance rebate, you are required to make an official request during your initial offer (we will cover details about the negotiation process later on). As your offer is submitted, you will be required to submit the course certificate as proof that you took the course.

vi) *Fannie Mae and Freddie Mac loans*

Then you have Fannie Mae and Freddie Mac loans. These are another great option for you if you are having a hard time coming up with a significant down payment, but still wish to buy a home.

These two agencies do not offer these loans; the agencies are only involved in providing liquidity for the housing market by purchasing mortgages in the secondary market, which they can hold on to, or securitize and sell off to Wall Street.

Given their role, these agencies just dictate the terms under which they are willing to purchase these mortgages. It is up to the lenders to stick to terms if they intend to sell these mortgages to these two agencies.

With this program, you are allowed to put up as little as 3% in down payment for the home that you intend to purchase, provided you or your partner can be classified as a first-time home-buyer.

There is also a **HomeStyle Renovation loan** that serves those who are willing to take on the risk of buying a fixer-upper property but can't afford the associated costs of fixing-up the home (fixer-upper properties will be detailed later).

vii) *Energy-Efficient Mortgage (EEM) Program*

Do you wish to purchase a home but hope to save on utility bills by making your home energy-efficient? You know, for instance, installing solar panels and relying on wind energy?

The good news is that there is a program that provides financing to cater for such home improvements. And that program is the Energy Efficient Mortgage Program (or EEM). It was introduced by the Department of Housing and Urban Development (HUD) in 1992 as a means of helping families cut costs on utility bills.

It works by stretching your Debt-to-Income ratio in such a way that you can qualify for a much bigger loan package that can cater for such home improvements.

EEM programs are available for conventional loans as well as for loans guaranteed by the government for first-time homebuyers such as FHA and VA.

It is important to note, though, that for you to qualify for these programs, a home energy rater has to conduct an assessment and prove to the lender that your home is indeed energy-efficient.

To find out whether your lender offers such a program, simply ask when applying for the loan.

viii) FHA Section 203 (K) Loan Program

If you have an eye for the potential of homes that need repair (or fixer-uppers as they are often called), especially those located in older neighborhoods, then you will be happy to find out that the government has a program that caters for your needs.

That program is the FHA Section 203 (k) loan. These loans are provided by conventional lenders but are backed by the FHA. The federal government backs these loans because, quite often, lenders are unwilling to offer financing to cover the cost associated with fixer-uppers due to the risk involved.

With this type of loan, the lender is able to provide you with a single loan package that is meant to cover both price of the fixer-upper property as well as the cost of renovating it. In some instances, the loan can even cover the cost of rent that you may incur as the property undergoes construction. Due to their special purpose, these loans are also called *construction loans*.

ix) Native American Direct Loan

Are you a Native American Veteran or a non-Native American married to a Native American? If so, then you will be happy to learn that the U.S Department of Veterans Affairs (VA) offers a loan that allows you to either buy, build, or improve a home that is located on federal trust land. That loan is the native American Direct Loan (NADL)

What's more, you also have the opportunity to refinance a mortgage on an existing loan if you hope to get a lower interest rate.

You may qualify for this loan if besides being a veteran who is either a native or married to a native, you meet these requirements:

- You have a valid VA Certificate Of Eligibility (COE)
- You meet the VA credit score requirements
- You can prove that you make enough to cover your mortgage payments
- You intend to live in the home

The benefits of obtaining this loan are:

- You get to enjoy a low fixed interest rate of 4.25%
- You won't be required to come up with any down payment
- You won't be required to pay Private Mortgage Insurance
- It's very easy to qualify for the loan
- The closing costs are small
- You can borrow up to the limit laid out by Fannie Mae and Freddie Mac
- You can borrow more than once in the future

2. About Private Mortgage Insurance

I have mentioned mortgage insurance countless times in the book so far. Perhaps you are wondering what it is all about and under what circumstances it applies. So let me clear up that issue.

First of all, understand that mortgage insurance is a requirement that helps the lender reduce their risk of loss should you default on your loan.

Mortgage insurance is usually required of those borrowers who pay less than 20% in down-payment when purchasing a home. When you pay such a low down-payment, the lender perceives a higher risk because such a low amount makes it a lot easier for you to walk away from the deal should any problem arise. This means that much of the risk will land on the shoulders of the lender.

Now, there are two instances when this can happen – when taking a government-backed loan such as FHA or USDA or when you take a conventional loan. In the first instance, the mortgage insurance is called Mortgage Insurance Premium (or MIP). In the case of conventional loans, it is called Private Mortgage Insurance.

Mortgage insurance is usually calculated as a percentage of the amount you borrow. In most cases, it is about 0.5% on an annual basis. This means if you take PMI on a 200,000 loan, then you will have to pay $1000 each year.

$$\frac{0.5\% \times 200{,}000}{100\%} = \$1000$$

That amount is usually divided by the number of months in a year and added to your mortgage payment. This means that you will pay roughly $83 each month in addition to your mortgage payment.

Keep in mind that most lenders require that you pay at least two months' worth of PMI at closing. So you should factor that in as part of the closing costs of your home.

Now, it is worth noting that mortgage insurance doesn't have to be paid throughout the life of the loan. If the equity in your home rises to say, 20%, you may request to have your insurance canceled.

For this to happen, your mortgage lender will require that your property be appraised to truly ascertain the claim that your equity in the home has actually risen, and by how much. You will also need to display consistency in making your mortgage payments.

3. About homeowner's insurance

Private mortgage insurance is very different from homeowners' insurance, which is a policy that you take on to cover losses caused by loss of assets on the property, damage to the property, or injury caused by accidents on the property.

The primary difference between this type of Insurance and PMI is that this one covers you. Therefore, it is in your best interest to get it.

Lenders will require that you show proof of possessing homeowners insurance before they can extend the necessary funds to finance the purchase of the home. They may offer to obtain such an insurance policy for you at an extra cost if you happen not to have any.

Just like PMI, this type of insurance payment is usually bundled together with your your mortgage payment at the end of the month.

4. Getting a pre-approval

Before you embark on the process of shopping for a deal on a home, you must obtain what is known as a pre-approval letter.

A pre-approval letter is a document showing the loan amount that a lender is willing to extend to you in the event that you come across a home that you decide to purchase.

Having this document comes in handy, especially in a competitive real estate market that guarantees that any seller will have multiple bids on an offer. This document shows your seriousness and commitment. A seller is more likely to consider your offer as opposed to someone who negotiates without any proof of purchasing power.

Now, there is one thing you have to keep in mind, though; pre-approval letters are way different from prequalification letters. The latter refers to a letter issued by a lender detailing how much you may qualify for, based on a verbal discussion. The lender does not take any steps to verify any facts you hand over to them.

Since there is no verification of financial health, prequalification letters usually carry less weight and therefore give you little advantage, if any. Going through the trouble to obtain a pre-approval letter can pay off handsomely.

Given that prequalification letters involve little to no work, and that they carry little importance, many lenders offer them for free. On the other hand, pre-approval letters involve plenty of legwork, and therefore, most lenders will charge you to write one.

Now you have enough knowledge to help you navigate your way through the process of securing financing. Next up, we talk about the home buying process from start to finish.

The Home Buying Process

So far, we've covered much of the preparation work you will need to carry out before you begin the process of purchasing a home. Now it is time we described the process itself, including what you will need to do at each step. This is where the rubber hits the road, so pay close attention.

Let's get started.

Step 1: Assembling The Right Team

This might come as a shock to you - especially if you have never done it before - but purchasing a home is a team effort.

Even with the help of a comprehensive book like this, there is still much that you will not know. Therefore, you will need to seek the services of competent professionals.

You see, purchasing a home is a complex transaction involving many different subject areas that are, by themselves, pretty difficult to grasp. And no matter how smart you may be, you will never have the time to become an expert at all of them.

What's more, if you happen to get some of these areas wrong, simply because you were incompetent, inexperienced, and unprofessional, you could get into some serious trouble. It's a lot smarter and economical to hire people who know what they are doing and let them do their job. Never do another man's job.

Now, we are going to look at the various professionals who will make up your team, and what kind of role each one will be playing. We will also look at the criteria you are going to use to vet each one of them so that you end up with top-shelf experts.

i)   You

The first and most important member of your house buying team is you. You are at the center of the action. You are the person who matters the most, as you are the boss.

Without you, none of the other members would exist. You are responsible for their paychecks. You are the one who calls the shots.

So, it helps to know everything you possibly can about the bigger picture of what you are doing. Managers and directors who run big corporations are responsible for steering the company in the right direction. They are responsible for developing insights such as industry trends, sustainable finance alternatives, the overall shape and health of the company, and so on.

This is the same role you assume when you become a house buyer. The first thing you do is understand the general picture.

What does the entire process look like? Where are the potential problem areas? How do things need to look like for things to be right?

That is what this book helps you with. The knowledge in this book helps you become a better supervisor to your team.

If you ignore your role, and what it calls for, then you will surely suffer the consequences. Other players on your team may skim money right under your nose due to your lack of understanding of what you are doing.

ii)   *Real estate agent*

The next member on your team is your real estate agent.

This is the expert who is very familiar with the local property prices and what is on the market. Your real estate agent is also familiar with what legal issues cover the properties in your prospective area and can advise you accordingly.

If you hire a good real estate agent, he or she should be able to find properties on your behalf, inform you of the prices, and negotiate the deal on your behalf. Those are the things you will be paying him to take care of.

If you are a busy person who spends much of your time on your job, then you can trust a top-gun real estate agent to handle most of the important work in securing you a home. A good real estate can even help you supervise other members on the team and oversee the entire home-buying process.

Since a real estate agent is such a valuable team player, it helps to know how you can evaluate and pick a good one. So let's spend some time talking about how you can do that.

Types of real estate agents

First, it helps to know that there are two types of real estate agents on the market. They are:

a) Seller's agents.

Seller's agents are simply there to represent the opposite side of your home purchase deal – the selling side.

They will advise and take care of the interests of the seller. These are the types of agents that you want to steer clear of. They don't have your interests at heart. At the very least, you can expect them to try and get you to spend a large sum of your money on your deal so that they can take home a bigger paycheck.

b) Buyer's agents

On the other hand, you have what is known as a buyer's agent.

This is the type of agent you should be looking for. The law stipulates that he or she takes care of your best interests.

Now, obviously, this type of agent will still have a conflict of interest even though he or she is on your team because their take-home pay is dependent on how much you spend on a property deal.

But, there is a neat trick that you can employ to incentivize this type of agent to act in your interest and find you the best deal possible.

Here it is: offer them a flat fee, and then offer a bonus on the side for every low price they can get you.

Let me explain.

Let's say that you have found a property that has been listed for $200K. And let's say that the agent you are working with typically takes home 3% ($6,000, split between both agents). You can agree to such an amount and then offer to pay $100 for every $1000 bargain on the deal.

Thus, you will have provided the agent with a financial motive to get you the lowest price he or she possibly can because he or she will pocket more money if they do so.

If this works out your favor, you can get a deal at $180K and pay $2000 in bonuses. You will have gotten a deal at 20K below fair market value and will have paid a low price for it. It's a classic win-win situation for both parties, and they all come out happy.

So how do you go about finding a quality real estate agent?

First of all, I must say that you will have to interview a number of them. This way, you can nail down your options to the best of the three. It will also force them to strive and show competence to win your business. Competition always makes the game fairer for the consumer. And this is what you want to start with.

I recommend checking out the local real estate companies and asking for the top-guns in their stables. Inform each one of your candidates that you will be evaluating them against their peers to find the best. It is better to be frank with them from the word go.

Ask them to show up to the interview with copies of their activity list. This is a document showing deals in which the agent participated in within the last 12 months. It should contain the following data:

- The addresses of the properties that were sold
- The types of properties the agent dealt in. Are they condos, single-family homes, or mansions?
- The asking prices of the properties
- The dates when the deals on the properties were closed

- The parties the agent represented. Did they represent the buying or selling side?

- The total value of deals closed

- The name, addresses, and contact details of the buyers and/or sellers.

This document is worth its weight in gold in the process of finding a real estate agent. It speaks volumes about the candidate you will be interviewing. It is a fact-sheet that will do much of the weeding out for you.

The first sign that you shouldn't be working with a certain agent is if he or she has problems producing their activity list. It may be a sign that they are hiding something ugly that they don't wish for you to discover. Drop them immediately and find a replacement that has nothing to hide. Honesty should be your first evaluation criterion.

After that, you can proceed with the interview process. Here are the most important questions that you will want to ask.

1. *Are you practicing full-time or part-time?*

The best real estate agents work full time. If your candidate is spending time doing something else and works part-time, then they are, probably, not competent enough.

Being an agent involves enough work without needing to do anything else. Serving you will take up a huge amount of time, so you should have no business with anyone working part-time.

2. Which side do you typically represent?

Is it the buyer side or the seller side?

The activity list should point this one out clearly. But it also helps if the agent speaks for him or herself. There should be consistency between what the agent tells you and what you see on paper.

3. Are you independent or do you work with a firm

Some agents work solo and some work with a firm. The firm may be a brokerage firm that takes a fee from the agent's sale, to shoulder responsibility for the agent's actions.

Find out what type of agent you are dealing with. There is no better variety when it comes to this. But, if the agent is part of a brokerage firm, you will have to do some more work to determine the reputation of the firm.

4. How long have you been practicing?

Generally, the more experience an agent has in the business, the better. But, you should pay attention to other factors as well. Experience alone should not be the sole decision-making factor.

5. Are you on any professional education program?

Serious professionals will seek to improve their level of competence by adding to their skillset. If you find that the candidate shows this quality, then that is a better sign as compared to one who doesn't.

6. How well do you understand my needs when it comes to choosing a home?

For you to ask this question, you ought to have explained your needs to the agent prior to the interview. This question is merely a way to assess his or her level of understanding of what you explained to them.

The agent should remember and summarise your needs accurately without leaving important points out. If they don't manage to do this, then you know that you are working with the wrong person.

7. What are the kind of properties that you specialize in?

This is very important; you want an agent that is familiar with your market. This pertains both to the property type as well as the price range.

If you are looking for a looking to buy a single-family bungalow in Dayton, Ohio, you may not want to work with a mega-star real estate agent who sells overpriced mansions in the most exclusive neighborhood in the area.

You want to work with someone who has specialized in the kind of properties that you hope to buy and that are within your price range. Anything outside your parameters is a complete *"No!"*

8. What do you think of your competing aspirants?

Evaluate what they think of their peers who are competing for your business. If they are competent professionals, their remarks ought to be good. The last thing you want to have is a real estate agent who is too egocentric to admit the presence of other equally competent professionals.

A good real estate agent should receive enough business without having to resort to primitive tactics such as destroying the reputation of a fellow hard-working competitor.

9. How many clients are you currently serving?

You also need to find out whether the agent has time to fit you into their schedule. You don't want to find out that the agent has spread himself too thin to the point where he or she will have problems serving you. So ask. If you discover that your agent is too preoccupied to the point of raising concerns, go with your gut and back out.

10. Are you in a partnership arrangement, or do you use assistants?

Some top agents may delegate time-consuming activities to assistants or partners. If that is the case, find out whether they are competent. Invite them to an interview, if you must, so that you have a good idea of what you will be dealing with. You don't want to hire an agent, only to end up spending most of the time dealing with an assistant who you don't seem to get along with.

11. Are there other important things that you think I should know of?

This is the agent's chance to raise any emergent issues that may be of concern. Are there important developments that you should know of?

Is the agent leaving his company to go solo next week? Is he taking a trip to the Bahamas next summer, and therefore hopes to close all deals before then? Is he sending his assistant on a compulsory leave?

You don't want unexpected surprises. So give the agent a chance to let you know of what lies ahead so that you are better prepared or seek better alternatives elsewhere.

iii) Lender

Home buying is a "pay to play" game.

The problem is, most people cannot afford to come up with all the money involved in the process. The amounts are staggering.

If you are like most people reading this book, you belong to the category of people who cannot afford to pay cash for your home. You need a partner; someone with the means, who can provide you with the cash you need for a small price. That partner is the lender.

A good lender will provide the loan products you need with attractive and competitive terms. A good lender may even help you find the right loan for you from a universe of loan products.

We talked about how you can evaluate a good lender in the previous chapter. Kindly revisit the material if you need more clarification on the matter.

iv) Property inspector

A home's value is also greatly tied to the state of its physical condition.

If a house is in tip-top condition, it will sell for a good price. If there are physical defects in the house, this should lower its value greatly. This is because it costs money to fix problems in a house that has problems.

That is the main reason why homes like fixer-uppers are lowly priced. We will talk about them later on when we cover ways to find a great deal on a property. But understand this; such homes involve the risk of losing money during repair depending on the extent of physical damage.

You can assess the extent of the damage done to a house simply by looking at it. In many cases, physical problems with houses are barely seen until much later on when it's already too late. For this reason, you never want to judge with your eyes.

Given the economic risk, it helps to have every inch of the house that you plan on buying, inspected by a professional.

So how do you go about finding a good property inspector? After all, just like agents, some may not be competent pros, as you may imagine. Inspection is one area where anybody who can dress up and act like an inspector will get inspection assignments.

Considering what is at stake here, you don't want to cheap out on the process of finding an inspector. It could cost you a small fortune down the road. Perform your due diligence and find a professional inspector.

First, ask around from friends and locals who have recently been involved in home purchases in the area. They should provide good leads. Also, ask your real estate agent to recommend some good ones. Chances are, they are familiar with quite a number of them.

After assembling a list of possible candidates, you should engage them in an interview, pretty much the same way we did when it involved agents.

Useful questions to ask should include the following:

1.   *Do you work full-time or part-time?*

You know the answer; professional inspectors make a living doing inspection only. This means that their entire livelihood is dependent on their fees. As such, they must and should work full-time.

2.   *How long have you been in the business?*

A consummate professional who knows what they are doing has at least a few years of practice under their belt.

3.   *Do you have errors and omissions insurance?*

This is a type of insurance cover that takes care of costs brought about by physical defects on the property that the inspector did not spot. As you can imagine, this type of insurance is a must for all professionals.

4. **How many inspections do you carry out in a year?**

You should expect a number ranging anywhere from 150 to 400.

5. **Are you familiar with the local market?**

You want to work with someone who is familiar with common problems in the area. For example, are there mudslides, floods, earthquakes? And if so, is he familiar with local laws and regulations regarding the standards of housing?

6. **Do you possess special certifications and licenses?**

A good inspector has a background in related fields such as architecture, construction, engineering, plumbing, electricity, insurance, and the like. These backgrounds can add special insights that can prove to add value to the inspector's skillset.

It also helps if the inspector is a member of the [American Society of Home Inspectors (ASHI)](). This is a professional body of qualified inspectors. Inspectors affiliated with this organization, have experience inspecting at least 250 properties, which is a good bottom-line that helps add credibility. If you pick a member of this body, your odds of ending up with a quality inspector go up significantly.

7. What will be the scope of your work?

A good inspector should tell you that they hope to cover structural and mechanical problems involving everything from the roof all the way to the foundation. Anything less than this is unacceptable.

8. Will you mind if I am present as you do your work?

A good inspector should insist that you be present.

9. Will you include an estimate of the cost it will take to correct mistakes spotted by your inspection?

This question is meant to determine whether the professional oversteps his boundaries and does things outside his or her scope of work. If an inspector says yes to this, disqualify them and move on to the next. Be wary of professionals who offer advice that isn't in line with what they do best.

10. Will you mind if I contact some of your previous customers?

A good inspector will have no problem with you contacting people they have served in the past because they have nothing to hide. They know that their quality of work is good.

Be sure to check with the customers to verify whether they'd recommend the inspector for another assignment.

v) *Escrow officer*

You also need an objective third-party to handle the financial side as well as the paperwork involving the transaction.

This is because there is always a lack of trust between the buyer and seller in transactions like these. A neutral third party always serves the purpose of some kind of referee to the process.

vi) *Tax advisor*

A tax advisor can advise you on local tax laws and also help you with deductible expenses involving the transaction. As such, he or she is also another important team player.

vii) *Lawyer*

A lawyer who specializes in real estate can also help iron out legal issues involving your transaction. You may not need this team player, but in instances where you feel uncomfortable about the complexity of the transaction, involving a lawyer can be a wise decision.

Now you know how to assemble robust team. Let's move on with discussing the rest of the steps in the process.

Step 2: Locating A Good Home Deal

Everyone loves a deal, right? When you walk into a car dealership, you don't expect to walk out having paid the sticker price, or do you? In the same way, when you hit the housing market, you want, at the very least, to find a great bargain on a good home.

But finding a great bargain can be challenging, especially if you don't know what you should be doing. After all, you have no experience in real estate; you are just a newbie.

This step will focus on giving you a simple crash course on finding a great deal. If you follow what is recommended within, you will hardly end up disappointed with your results.

So let's get to it.

Principles To Keep In Mind

First, you need to grasp some basic principles that govern the whole deal locating process in the housing markets.

These principles are the foundation that governs everything else. Violate them, and you'll almost surely end up with a bad deal. Follow them, and you'll find a great deal on any property.

Here they are:

i) *The principle of progression*

The principle of progression states that cheaper houses on the market are usually enhanced in value by more expensive properties that surround them.

This means that whenever you are shopping for a home, finding the cheaper houses in a neighborhood of more expensive homes is a much better path to success.

In other words, if you happen to find a deal on a home going for $180,000 in a neighborhood of homes going for as much as $200,000 to $250,000, you should consider taking it.

Why?

Because the surrounding homes are likely to pull up its value. Keep in mind that in real estate, homes tend to retail at a price that is similar to those that is around them.

So, this is the first thing you will need to keep in mind when shopping for a deal.

ii) *The principle of regression*

The principle of regression is simply the exact opposite of the principle of progression.

It states that the more expensive homes in a neighborhood are usually pulled down in value by the cheaper ones.

Thus, a $300,000 home in a neighborhood of $250,000 homes is going to do much poorly in the ensuing years.

With this in mind, you must never go for the most expensive homes in a neighborhood, no matter what. It is just not worth it.

You might reason that, it's pretty common sense not to violate this rule, but people break this rule every time.

You see, wherever emotions are involved, common sense is frequently thrown out of the window. And home buying is one area where people let emotions trump logical reasoning.

For instance, you might choose to buy the $350,000 home in that neighborhood because you wish to flaunt your status and please everybody else. Or, you may be impressed by the design and the size, which leads you to reason that paying more is a great deal.

But the truth is, if your goal is to find a great deal because you hope to sell the house for profit someday, it is prudent to let the lousy opportunity pass. In the end, the cheaper houses in the neighborhood will make it less desirable, and people will bid much lower prices for this home.

iii) *The principle of conformity*

The principle of conformity simply states that you should be looking to buy houses that are prototypical in an area. Therefore, if bungalows characterize the neighborhood, trying to buy a ranch-style home is a bad idea. Also, if the houses in the area are primarily old, buying a new one is not likely to be a great deal.

If you buy a house that is "too unique" simply because it fits your unique tastes and style, you will be likely disappointed to find that it wasn't such a great deal after all.

In general, the home that you buy should have the same standards as others on the block in terms of the following characteristics:

- *Age* - Only buy a new home in a neighborhood of new homes and vice versa.

- *Style* – Never buy a house that sticks out like a sore thumb in a neighborhood of homes that almost look the same.

- *Condition* – Go with the trend. Let the neighborhood set the standards. If you try to renovate too much, you might end up with the most expensive house on the block, which will never attract a good price when you consider selling.

Now that you have the principles under your belt, let's look at some nice candidates for great property deals.

a) New vs. Used homes

You probably made your choice regarding this matter when we talked about requirements earlier in this book. But most people are not sure when it comes to this issue. It can be pretty confusing.

Is a newer home better than a used one? Which one is likely to be a great deal?

To this, I feel that the answer is, "Both." Any can be a great deal, and it all comes down to preferences. Some people will prefer older homes, and others will prefer newer ones.

The key is to shop with the previously discusses principles in mind. If you follow them, you should have an easier time finding a great deal.

That said, to make an informed decision, you are better off knowing the advantages and disadvantages associated with both new and used homes.

Let's start with new homes.

Advantages of new homes

- They are built to fit more current standards. Therefore, they will be easier to sell to the younger generation.

- They are cheaper to maintain right from the start. Older homes may require constant repairs and renovations that cost quite a bit of money. You don't have that problem with new homes.

- They easily fit a modern lifestyle. You will not have to adapt your lifestyle to fit the home. Newer homes come with standard features like Jacuzzis, enough wall to accommodate plasma TVs, internet connections, computers, and so on. Achieving this with much older houses that were not built with such facilities in mind can be a lot harder. You might even have to forgo such things.

Disadvantages of new homes

- It costs a lot of money to decorate and furnish new homes.

- Most prices are not up for negotiation. Developers often look to maintain the value of their property on the market; they feel that bargaining the price is a bad idea. They may agree to offer extras like free carpets and so on, but the price may not be something they are willing to discuss.

- New homes are generally more costly than when compared to used ones on a square-per-foot basis. This might be because land, materials, and labor is a lot more expensive than it was years ago.

- If a new home is built in a more developed area, it could be on undesirable land. This is because earlier developers tend to grab the best land. Afterward, the remaining land in the area now becomes the prime real estate.

And now, let's talk about the used homes.

Advantages of used homes

- They are a lot cheaper than new ones. Used homes outnumber the new ones on the market. The basic law of demand and supply makes their prices gravitate towards the lower end. Also, they cost a lot less to construct less during their era. So they generally sell for less.

- Their prices are usually negotiable. The sellers of these homes know that they have competition, and most usually aren't interested in keeping the value of the home in the market constant, so they are open to negotiation.

- The neighborhoods are more established. You often have a good idea of the quality of the neighborhood you are getting into because time has proven it to you. With new homes, you are always gambling with an uncertain future.

- Used homes have been time-tested. Only time tells how a house is going to age. With new homes, it's only a wait and see situation. What if the wall starts to wear off after 5 years of occupancy? What if the wooden doors start to change shape due to humidity after 10 years?

- The craftsmanship in older homes is usually more artistic. In today's housing markets, getting such work done can be quite costly.

Disadvantages of used homes

- They cost more to maintain. They have been subjected to wear and tear over the years and will most likely need constant repairs and improvements - money that is supposed to come out of your pockets.

- Some of their features may be obsolete
- At times, they can be located in undesirable neighborhoods.

You will have to carefully weigh your choices based on what you now know about new and used homes and arrive at a reasoned conclusion.

b) Homes that are part of a foreclosure

Typically, when you get a home through a mortgage, and you are unable to pay the loan, the lender usually forecloses on the home to get its money back.

Foreclosure simply means repossessing the house and offering it up for auction so that money can be quickly recovered.

Sometimes (but not always), homes that are back on the market due to foreclosure can be great deals. But you have to be careful with them because many issues tend to surround these types of properties.

For instance, a few issues regarding foreclosure properties on auction might include:

- Vandalized properties by previous occupants. Previous occupants are not usually all too happy when their property gets repossessed and sold off. You may acquire a property that has been damaged severely, requiring you to fund some major renovations.

- It is important to note that you are not usually allowed to inspect the home before the auction. So, you are usually gambling with the physical condition of the house.

- If you acquire the property on auction, the liabilities of the previous occupant of the property become yours. Sometimes, these liabilities may be huge if the previous occupants were irresponsible and even borrowed against the equity on the home.

- Sometimes the previous occupants are reluctant to leave the property willingly. You have to go through the trouble of evicting them. At times, you may encounter armed resistance.

- Given the substantial risk involving auctioned foreclosure properties, many lenders are usually unwilling to finance these purchases. So unless you are wealthy and can afford to pay cash, lenders won't be willing to back you on such a risky deal.

Suffice to say, foreclosure properties on auction are usually wild bets that offer you very little opportunity to control risk.

So, what is the right way to purchase a property that was part of a foreclosure? It's quite simple. Buy it directly from a lender who acquired the title to the property simply because no one else could buy it during the auction phase.

Here are some reasons why I consider this to be the path that involves the least amount of risk:

- Undisclosed debt obligations, legal claims on assets, and court rulings are either written off and dismissed or revealed before you make a decision.

- The lender allows you to inspect the house before purchase.

- The lender is usually willing to work with you and to even negotiate terms under which the property is sold. For instance, a lender may knock off a certain amount of the price due to damages to the property. They may also extend credit to cater for repairs to damages on the property.

Sometimes such deals may be good because lenders often prefer to get rid of such properties so that they can focus on their main business of lending. Nevertheless, I strongly insist that you proceed with a lot of caution when considering purchasing foreclosure properties.

c) *Fixer-upper homes*

Then you have a category of homes called fixer-uppers.

These are homes that are good, but not excellent physical conditions. They may require a few repairs for them to meet the standards set by the neighborhood. Real estate agents frequently refer to them as "handy-man specials," "needing work," or "of great potential."

It takes a person with a vision and an appetite for risk to purchase homes like these. I say that they involve risk because you usually won't find all fixer-uppers to be great deals. Some can turn out to be money-pits.

It's important to keep in mind that fixer-uppers are only attractive during rising markets. If the market is moving too slowly or even taking a nosedive, the risk associated with fixer-uppers becomes substantially significant and almost pointless, unless you are a real estate veteran.

So, for you to mitigate some of that risk and possibly land a deal of a lifetime, I will list several things that you are supposed to consider when purchasing this type of home.

Here they are:

- First of all, ensure that you adhere to the principles that we talked about in the beginning. Make sure that the surrounding properties in the area are more expensive than the one that you have your eyes on. Your real estate agent should provide this information.

- Second, make sure that the home is located in a quality neighborhood. If you did your homework on what makes a good neighborhood as suggested earlier in this book, then this shouldn't be a problem. High-quality neighborhoods have certain very common features. Make sure they are present.

- Third, be sure to find out whether the cost of renovating the property will be fully compensated by the value of the homes around.

To do this, ask for quotations from suppliers and contractors who will be needed to do the work of renovating the house. Use this figure to negotiate an acceptable price with the seller.

The total amount on the quotations should be equal to or significantly less than the difference between the agreed price with the seller and the average selling price of the nearby properties as estimated by your agent.

If this amount is greater than zero, negotiate further or move on to another property. The last thing you want is a renovation cost that will end up making your house the most expensive one in the entire neighborhood.

It's good to have an idea of what kind of problems are worth fixing when it comes to fixer-uppers and which ones aren't. Therefore, let's talk about them for a minute,

1. *Structural repairs*

Structural repairs have a lot to do with the physical structure of the house. They may involve things like fixing a roof (or installing a completely new one), fixing drainage pipes, taking care of problems with the foundation, and installing a new electrical system.

These kinds of repairs take up huge amounts of money, and they usually have little impact on the house's overall value. The home you consider buying should have very few of these kinds of problems or none at all; otherwise, it's a major risk for you.

2. *Renovations*

Then you have renovations. These are modifications to a house that are supposed to make it look more modern. They make a home look a lot better, and people can notice the changes. For instance, fixing a bathroom, applying new paint, landscaping, redesigning the kitchen, and so on fall under this category.

Renovations, when compared to structural repairs, are much cheaper and more desirable, both in your eyes and in the eyes of potential buyers. These are the type of problems that are usually worth solving. Structural repairs can sometimes amount to building a new house entirely, which is never a good idea.

So there you have it. Now you know how (and under what circumstances) you will choose to work fixer-uppers to your advantage. If done correctly, in the years to come, a fixer-upper can pocket you a size-able profit.

d) Back on the Market (BOM) homes

Lastly, you can also find great deals in BOM homes.

These are homes that were once taken off the market when a deal was taking place, but suddenly got listed back on the market after the deal failed to materialize.

Buyers always view such properties with a lot of skepticism. They often speculate over what could have gone wrong for a desirable house to get back on the market.

As a result of this skepticism, demand for the home falls, and consequently, the price is usually adjusted downwards to match buyer sentiment.

If you take it upon yourself to investigate the reasons for the deal on a BOM property falling apart, you may land a great deal.

Frequently, deals fall apart because the parties involved fail to agree over how costs associated with fixing problems uncovered during the inspection would be shared. In other cases, it can be due to worse issues, in which case you may choose to step aside.

But, if the issue turns out to be the former, you can actually ask for the inspection reports and decide for yourself whether the risk is worth taking. Sometimes, you may find that the house is a fixer-upper that is worth fixing, and you end up landing a great deal. Just be sure to follow the instructions we talked about regarding fixer-uppers, and you will be fine.

Step 3: Having The Home Inspected

The next course of action in the process is getting your prospective home inspected.

You owe yourself this one. Purchasing a home is a big-ticket purchase, probably the biggest one you will ever make in your family. And if you want to protect what may end up being your largest single financial investment in life, then you better make sure you have your property inspected.

Have you ever made a small financial mistake? Maybe you bought something that you thought was good, only to find that it was a fake? Or perhaps you poured a small fortune into some shady investment opportunity that you were pitched to by some internet guru?

Do you remember the pinch? How badly it hurt to lose even a small amount of your hard-earned money in such a spectacular fashion?

Now imagine repeating the same mistake, only on a much bigger scale. It could destroy you.

Think of it this way; you go out searching for a house and land a great deal. You visit the premises, and you are impressed. You want the home right away. The charming seller convinces you that the house is completely new… And that it was inspected by an expert, right before it was listed on the market.

The seller even shows you a portfolio of houses that he has dealt in, in the past. You being the naïve and trusting person that you are, love the pitch. You get sold immediately.

You think to yourself, "What could go wrong? The house is new, and this guy seems legit and experienced?" You had planned to spend $350 on inspection fees, but now you are happy to keep your money. "I'll buy me a stake and get some treats for my golden retriever when this is all done," you say to yourself, smiling.

Everything seems okay, and in a month, you've moved in. In two months or so, you discover a crack so huge on the wall of your kitchen pantry, you could stick a pencil in it. You are worried and shocked beyond belief; you rush out to find some help on the matter. You consult a building contractor in town who shows up and, after a few hours of inspecting the issue, informs you of the terrifying news. The problem is structural and very serious. If not taken care of from the foundation, the wall could collapse. The total cost of the operation could cost you a staggering $35,000!

Wow! Now you have to spend 100 times more than you tried saving? You charge the whole thing up to your credit card, and before you know it, you are in the financial hole.

Can you see why inspections are so important? You must conduct them on any property, no matter what the condition is. And with experts of your own choosing.

What Will Your Inspector Be Looking For?

So, what will your inspector be looking for?

It helps to know that there can be two kinds of defects that a property can have, and your inspection should help you turn them up. They are:

i)   *Patent defects*

These are problems that you can spot yourself because you can see with your own eyes; issues like leaky faucets, water-stained walls, cracks, broken taps, and the like.

You don't need a trained eye to spot these problems. But you do need a professional to interpret their significance. For instance, how serious is that crack on the wall? Does it pose a serious threat? What can be done about it?

ii)   *Latent defects*

Latent defects are out of plain sight. The naked eye cannot see them because often, they are behind walls. Often, they are the most serious ones. A competent inspector should be able to spot them for you.

Think about problems like faulty wiring, cracked gas pipes, wood that has been infested by termites, cracked heat exchangers; these problems cannot be easily spotted, but obviously, they are disasters waiting to happen.

This is one of the many reasons why you cannot skip inspection under any circumstances.

With that knowledge under your belt, let us look at the type of inspections you will most likely consider.

Inspection Packages To Consider

i)   *Pre-purchase interior and exterior-components inspection*

This type of property inspection should be done on any property. It covers both outside and inside components of the house.

Here are just but a few areas that this inspection should target.

- The kitchen
- Insulation
- Gutters
- The roof
- The plumbing
- Smoke detectors
- Electrical systems
- Heating and cooling systems
- The foundation

What's more, the property inspector should also report on the health, safety, as well as environmental issues concerning the property.

Typically, this type of inspection is pretty comprehensive and takes up a lot of time. It usually takes up several hours and varies depending on how large the house you want to buy could be.

Sometimes, issues may arise from this type of inspection, which may prompt the inspector to advise a deeper investigation by more skilled experts.

Fees for this inspections can be expected to range anywhere from $350 to $600

ii) *Pest-control inspection*

This is an option that is especially important to you if you intend to occupy a home that is made of wood or that contains many wooden components.

Pests, especially in warmer areas, tend to attack wood, and homes made of wood are especially at high risk. Insects such as termites can eat through wood and put an entire structure at risk of falling. Others like carpenter ants, dry rot fungi, and powder post beetles are equally dangerous.

You need to request a specialist in wood inspection to figure out whether you face any major threats and what can be done about them.

Such inspections are of smaller scope and will, therefore, take you back $250 to $400.

iii) Architect's/General contractors inspection

You need this type of inspection done if you intend to carry out some corrective work or major renovations in properties such as fixer-uppers.

Perhaps you want to add a new bedroom so that your house matches what is in the rest of the neighborhood. You will need an expert opinion as to whether such a project is doable, and whether it will meet local legal requirements. In addition to that, you will need an estimated cost of the project.

This type of inspection should deliver the goods. But, it is important to keep in mind that this is not the type of inspection that helps you decide whether the home is a good buy or not. The previous two may are a better fit for that.

If you are the controlling type who wants to go over some of the inspection details on your own, I have taken the liberty to include a checklist that can help you go over some important items as you visit different properties.

House Inspection Checklist

Item	N/A	Yes	No	Comments
The doors and windows				
Doors open and close smoothly				
Hinges, screws, locks, handles, latches, stoppers, etc. are fitted properly, and have no rust				
The doors and windows move smoothly and with ease				
No broken glass				
The door frame is not bent				
When closed, the leads and the frames of the doors are aligned				
When closed, the gaps separating the doors and				

the frames are kept constant			
When closed, the gaps separating the floor and the doors is kept constant			
There are no scratch marks and cracks that can easily be spotted			
The painting, as well as varnishing, has been done uniformly			
All the faces of the doors are varnished			
There is no evidence of excessive paintbrush marks			
Outside			
There is proper drainage outside the house			
There is no stagnant			

water outside				
The leech field or septic tanks are not leaking				
The trees, the yard, and the landscape are in good shape				
No tree branches or small bushes are touching the house, or hanging from the rooftop				
The railings on the decks and the staircase are secure				
The patio, the driveway, the sidewalk, and even the entrance, are well placed away from the house				
The structure itself				
The sides of the house are straight, and not sagging, or bent.				

The window and door frames have a square-shaped appearance				
The part of the foundation that is visible looks straight, has no cracks and appears to be in good condition generally				
The surfaces on the outside				
Enough distance between the wooden ground siding (at least 6 inches)				
There are no cracks, rot, or decay on the siding				
There are no dents or damage to the aluminum siding				
The paint has no flaking or blisters				
There are no ugly stains				

The Attic				
No presence on the underside of the roof				
No decay or damage to structures				
Presence of insulation that is properly installed				
No presence of appliance, plumbing and exhaust vents terminating there				
No presence of open electrical splices				
Properly ventilated				
The Interior				
The walls, the floors, and ceilings have a straight appearance				
There is no presence of stains on the walls, the floor, or the ceilings				

The material on the flooring is in good condition			
The panel and wall covering is in good condition			
Wooden trim is in good condition			
Properly functioning switches and lights			
Sufficient electrical sockets in every room			
The sockets function properly			
Presence of heating and cooling system in each room that is habitable			
The insulation on walls is adequate			
The fireplace is in good condition			

The Kitchen				
An exhaust fan that is working and that has vents pointed outside the building				
A Ground Fault Circuit Interrupter, for sockets, located close to the sink				
Water drains properly through the dishwasher with no evidence of leaking				
The flooring cabinet under the sink has no presence of stains or decay				
The water drains through the sink properly				
The taps function properly				
The waste pipes are not excessively rusted or				

deteriorated			
The cabinets are in good condition			
The Bathrooms			
The exhaust functions properly and doesn't vent into the attic			
All the fixtures present have adequate flow and pressure			
The tub, the sink, as well as the shower drain properly			
Metal sinks show no presence of rust, and also don't leak			
The toilet functions properly			
The toilet appears to be stable, doesn't rock and has no presence of stains			

close to the base				
The tiles on the shower and tub are firmly secure, and the wall is firm				
No stains or leakage at the base of the shower				
The Plumbing				
There is no evidence of leakage or stains on visible pipes				
The water heater has no rust and is properly vented				
The water pump functions properly and doesn't short cycle				
Pipes that are galvanized do not restrict the flow of water				
Hot water has a temperature that ranges from 118 to 125 degrees				

Fahrenheit				
The Electrical system				
Visible wires are well secured and protected				
The fuses and circuit breakers do not overheat				
Branch circuits are not equipped with aluminum cable				
The Heating or Cooling system				
Operates well				
No presence of rust around the cooling unit				
No detectable odor from the combustion of gas				
The air filters are clean				
There is no asbestos on water pipes, air ducts, and heating pipes				

These details should give you an idea of what the professional will be looking at. As you go around the homes you are viewing, you can use the checklist to get a feel of how much 'work' may be required.

Now you know the details to help you navigate the inspection process. Next, we look at how you can negotiate to land a better deal on the price.

Step 4: Negotiating the deal

The great thing about shopping for real estate is that you just don't have to show up and pay the sticker price. When you show up at a grocery store, or at the supermarket, you simply grab the item and pay at the counter. If you hang around to haggle, you run the risk of embarrassing yourself. This is a widely accepted reality in society.

But dealing with homes is different; everything and anything involved in the process is negotiable. You can negotiate the asking price, the fees charged by inspectors, the real estate agents, whether or not the seller will pay closing costs, and so much more.

Unless you are the rare individual who prefers not to hang around bargaining for lower prices, you will want to know what you can do to make a deal look better than it first did.

This step is going to look at how a typical negotiation process looks like and what negotiation strategies can be employed. So let's begin.

Making Your First Offer

The first thing that you, as a prospective home buyer, will need to do in a typical transaction process is to prepare and submit your first offer. This is the first lowest price that you are willing to pay for the property, and that you hope the seller will gladly accept.

Now, before we go into details about how you may come up with that first price, you must keep one thing in mind; on many occasions, you will need to handle the process using documents.

By this, I mean that the first price you come up with will have to be written down in a contract document of some sort, detailing the terms and conditions under which that offer is applicable. Then, that document is sent to the seller, who will then have to go over it and send a reply.

In the past, this was a long and arduous task that involved a lot of patience. Today, things have been made a lot better by technology. These days, we have digital signing technology. The documents can be presented to you for signing digitally (such as via a tablet), and immediately sent to the seller who goes over them digitally as well.

This has significantly improved the process, and negotiations today can typically take a few days at most, depending on the needs of the parties involved.

Back to our discussion. So how do you go about determining that initial offer price?

Here are a few things that you will have to consider:

i) *How much have other homes in the area sold?*

This is one of the best methods you could use to come up with an initial offer. Simply look at the median selling price of similar homes in the area within the last six months.

If your real estate agent is competent enough, he or she should be able to provide you with this information.

As you compare the selling prices of comparable properties, be sure to check that they are indeed similar to yours. They have to be representative if you want the basis of your negotiation to be reasonable.

ii) *The seller's circumstances*

It pays a lot to do extensive homework on your seller.

The more you get to know about him or her, the better. This information can help you to negotiate much more effectively because you will know the right buttons to push.

Here's what I mean:

Suppose you find out that your seller is putting the house on the market because he or she is in financial trouble? What if you find out that he has a baby coming through in a few months and wants to be prepared? What if you learn that he or she got a job offer in another state or country and therefore is in a hurry to sell?

Knowing important bits of information like these puts you in a position of power. You know what makes the seller tick, and you can use that as a bargaining chip.

Time has shown that sellers are willing to agree to a much lower price than the asking price if one or more of these circumstances prevail in their lives?

- A house has been on the market for too long, and there has been little or no interest in it
- The price has had to be adjusted downwards at least once
- The seller has had to work with multiple agents in the past
- A recent deal on the property fell apart
- The seller is in a hurry to move and even has a specific date to do so

- The seller is experiencing a major life change such as retirement, divorce, or some other equally important development that has huge financial implications

- Rents in the area have been going down drastically, and the property you are looking at has served the role of being an investment property

- The seller is planning to use the proceeds of the sale to finance the purchase of a new home elsewhere.

You owe it to yourself to dig up as much as you can on the seller so that you can have some leverage on them.

iii) The market environment

The offers that you can make also depend on the market environment. Who does it favor? Is it you? Or is it the seller?

Generally, there are two types of housing market environments:

1. *A buyer's market*

This is a market that favors buyers.

It is a market in which the number of properties on the market is huge, as compared to willing buyers. This creates a situation where there is little demand for housing. Most sellers will have a hard time making sales during such a market. And since many of them have debts to service and bills to pay, desperation kicks in. This forces them to sell at lower prices, and therefore prices fall.

If you are negotiating in such a market, then you are in a position of power and should get a much, much better deal.

2. *A seller's market*

The opposite of a buyer's market is a seller's market.

Here, the number of buyers outnumbers that of sellers. It's open season for sellers because such a market favors their side. You will be competing amongst your fellow buyers, and each of you will have to quote a better price than the other. These constant bidding wars drive the prices of houses up.

In such a market, your offer has to be above the quoted price, so that you can convince the seller that you have the best possible deal for him or her.

Now, even though seller's markets drive home prices upwards, it doesn't mean that you should overstretch yourself. Be sure to quote prices that are well within your budget. Also, keep in mind that if you agree to a ridiculously high price on a property, a lender may reject your mortgage application.

A lender will have to send an appraiser to determine the value of the home and if the report comes in stating that the property is valued at a much lower price, you will either have to come up with the excess amount yourself or lose the mortgage deal altogether.

iv) Your agent's opinion

This is one of those instances where your agent becomes very useful. Provided you have incentivized him or her to find you the best deal possible, he or she should help you come up with a good starting offer price.

No matter what the current market environment, an experienced agent will have a fairly good idea of what a home ought to sell for, and his or her input becomes very valuable at this point.

Once you agree on an initial offer, write the amount on the contract document and send it over. Once your seller receives your offer, you will be faced with one of the three outcomes listed below.

Outcome 1: The seller counters your offer

If the seller feels that you have quoted a price that doesn't meet his or her expectations, they may respond with a counteroffer. A counteroffer from the seller will simply be a higher price than the one you quoted, and that the seller feels is much reasonable.

If you don't feel that the counteroffer is from the seller is acceptable, you can counter with an offer of your own. And the process will repeat itself for as long as it is necessary until both parties arrive at an acceptable middle ground.

Outcome 2: The seller rejects your offer

If you bid too low to the point where the seller feels offended, he or she will simply reject your offer outright. This could also happen if seller has already received an offer that he or she has already agreed to. Reasons for rejecting your offer may vary, and a seller usually has every right to keep them to him/herself.

Outcome 3: The seller accepts your offer

If the seller feels that your proposition is acceptable, he or she will accept your offer. In many cases, this usually happens after negotiations have taken place for some time. It rarely happens after you send in your initial offer.

Once your offer has been accepted, you will be required to sign a contract document that officiates the agreement between you and the seller. This contract document will contain many things pertaining the deal. A few items include:

- Associated fees and the party responsible for taking care of each cost
- Agent commissions and the manner in which they will be shared between them
- The selling price agreed between you and the seller

- The amount required in earnest money. Earnest money is the money that you pay the seller as a sign of good faith. It is meant to solidify the trust between you and the seller because it shows that you are actually interested in getting through with the purchase.

If you back out of the deal soon after paying the earnest money, the seller will have to penalize you for wasting their time and opportunity for landing other deals.

- The down payment on the purchase as well as the amount to be acquired through financing

- The terms of the loan that you will be obtaining to finance the rest of the purchase

- Contingencies on the accepted offer

- The rights afforded to the buyer of the property

- The escrow agent to act as referee in the deal

- The closing date

Contingencies

Once your offer has been accepted and you have agreed to sign the contract document, it is important that you include contingencies that offer you some reasonable exit terms in case unforeseeable circumstances come up in the near future. Let's talk about some contingencies that you should consider including:

i) *Financing contingency*

The first type of contingency that you want to have in place is one that has to do with financing.

You want to state that the offer is valid only if the mortgage loan you applied for goes through, and you receive the money. That way, if you don't receive financing, you remain protected against being heavily penalized by the seller.

ii) *Appraisal contingency*

You also want your offer to be valid contingent on appraisal.

This contingency keeps you from getting into trouble if it turns out that the house is grossly overpriced. It offers you the option of either negotiating the price downwards should the report come instating a lower amount, or backing out of the deal altogether. Obviously, this is very important.

iii) *Inspections*

If you wish to back off from purchasing a home that has serious and costly structural problems, then including this contingency on your contract is a must.

This rule applies to both old and new homes. The fact that a home hasn't had previous occupants doesn't mean that serious defects may be lacking. Often, developers take shortcuts during construction to cut their costs, and the finished house ends up having problems, which you, as the buyer, will end up paying to fix them.

If it turns out that the house has defects, the seller can offer to knock off the price, or bear the costs involved in construction. At times, the damage to the property is so bad, and you may have to walk out of the deal.

iv) *Attorney Review*

If you have a lawyer present on your team, then you will also want to include a contingency that offers him/her the chance and the time to go through the contract to ascertain that your best interests are represented in the document.

v) *Review of the preliminary title report*

You also want to make sure that there are no liens or other issues regarding the title of the property you intend to buy. Otherwise, you could face some serious legal issues down the road when unrecognized parties show up claiming rights to the property.

For this reason, you also want to make your offer contingent on your attorney reviewing the history of the title for a period of up to 50 years, to ensure that there are no pending legal issues associated with it.

vi) *Homeowner's insurance*

You also want to be certain that you will be able to obtain homeowner's insurance. This is important, not only because it covers you in the case of an incident occurring, but because many lenders make obtaining insurance a requirement before they extend you credit.

If, for some reason, you are unable to obtain homeowner's insurance, perhaps because there have been multiple past insurance claims filed, then you want to protect your interests and back out.

Once you have the above contingencies in place, you can then feel confident to proceed to the next step, which also happens to be the last one.

Step 5: Closing The Deal

After such an exhaustive process, if everything goes right, you will finally arrive at the final step – the moment where you finally close the deal and obtain keys to your new home. So, let's look at what usually happens during this step.

The first thing that happens is that your attorney and real estate agent work with you to make sure that you tick off contingencies included in the contract that were meant to protect you from unforeseen circumstances.

Removing these contingencies means that you are satisfied that your terms regarding them have been met, or that you have worked out the emergent issues with the seller to your satisfaction.

After that has happened, your attorney will work with you to help you acquire what is known as title insurance. This is insurance that protects you from issues regarding the title to the property, which the title search process may not have uncovered.

Once you have obtained title insurance, you will then proceed to the closing date. On this date, all parties involved in the deal will show up to an office to sign the contract forms that make the deal official.

It is at this point where you will also have to take care of closing costs. You already know about some of them, but for your own convenience, I thought it would be better to give you a complete picture of what costs you should expect to deal with. So here is a detailed list of the most common closing costs.

Closing Costs You Should Expect

1. Mortgage application fees

This fee will be demanded by your lender for the work involved in processing your loan. There usually isn't a set figure but, you can expect it to cost anywhere from $200 to $400.

Keep in mind that not all lenders will charge the same amount. Some will be more expensive than others. It is also worth noting that some lenders will demand that you pay this amount ahead of closing.

2. Appraisal fees

You will recall that I have pointed out on many occasions that your lender will look to protect his or her financial interests at all costs. One of the ways they make sure of that is by being certain that they are not lending you more money for the purchase of your home than it is worth.

To accomplish this, they will send a professional to do this kind of homework for them, and the bill will be on your tab. That professional is the appraiser. So expect to see this fee itemized on the disclosure forms on the day of closing. A good estimate would be around $100 to $400.

3. Inspection fees

For you to buy a home that is in great physical condition, an expert called an inspector has to verify that this the case. Depending on the depth of the work required, the amount, in this case, will range from $150 to $400.

4. Surveyors fee

This fee may not always be mandatory.

But, in some instances where the lender has reason to be concerned about the future disputes concerning the boundaries of your property, a professional surveyor may be called in to check that details are, in fact, well noted.

A rough estimate of $300 to $500 should be kept in mind in this case.

5. Legal fees

Home transactions can get pretty complicated, and there is often a lot of paperwork involved. More importantly, the nature of the terms contained in the documents you will be signing will need to be well understood.

A good lawyer can come in handy during these moments, and I seriously advise that you consider bringing one along. If you do, you will need to compensate him or her. Of course, lawyers are an expensive bunch, so you should expect to part with anything from $300 to $600.

6. Title search and insurance fees

You will need to iron out the details regarding the ownership history of the property so that you can avoid unwelcome surprises from people who may not have been consulted on the sale.

You also want to check whether other parties have a claim on the property – for instance, building contractors, suppliers, or even the government (tax liens).

A title search should be able to uncover whether most of these issues exist. But title searches are never perfect, and some details may be left out. This, therefore, calls for title insurance to be taken.

Both of these items cost money, and the amount will be included in closing costs. Expect to pay $150 to $200 in title search fees, and about 1% of the market value of the home in title insurance.

7. Private Mortgage Insurance

The traditional requirement from most reputable lenders is that you put up a down payment of 20% on your home before they can finance the rest. This generally meant to ensure that you have enough financial interest and commitment in the property and that you will not walk away at the first sign of trouble.

However, if you come up short, and you end up raising less than that amount (say 10%), then you will need to obtain Private Mortgage Insurance so that the lender feels protected.

Now, in many cases, PMI will amount to 2.5% of the mortgage amount. However, this amount is typically affected by other factors such as your credit history and score, the price of your home, the down payment you made, and so on. A portion of this amount will need to be paid at closing.

8. Homeowner's insurance

Another type of insurance that you will need is the one that covers you as the homeowner against damages at your own home. Almost all lenders will require that you have it.

The first year's premium required by this type of insurance will need to be paid at closing.

9. Prepaid interest

If you close on your home in the middle of the month at a time when your first mortgage payment is due, the lender will have to calculate the interest on the remaining days and charge the amount up at closing.

10. Points

We talked about points earlier. We saw how they are just yet another fee associated with processing your loan and are charged as a percentage of the loan amount. So, 1 point on a $200,000 loan amounts to $2,000.

If you agree to a loan that has points, expect the amount to be included as part of the closing costs.

11. Escrow fees

The referee who will preside over the financial details of the transaction and ensure that both parties honor their commitments will be the escrow agent. And as a professional, he or she will need to be compensated. Typically, 3 months' worth of escrow fees is usually included as part of the closing costs.

12. Realty transfer taxes

Yes, taxes are part of the equation too. Just in the same way you pay taxes when you purchase a new car, you should expect to pay taxes when you acquire a new home. The amount will be dependent on the value of the property, and the state your future home is located in.

13. Recording fees

The government will have to record your transaction in its books, and that will cost money too. Expect to pay $40 to $60 for this in most cases.

14. Prorated expenses

These refer to expenses associated with your home, such as homeowner association fees, condo fees, water, and so on. Depending on the time of the year, when you purchase your home, you will be expected to foot in your portion of the costs. Of course, fees like these can always be negotiated with the seller.

You will be expected to meet each cost, and depending on your agreement with the seller, he or she may cover some of them. By most estimates, they usually amount to anywhere between 2% and 5% of the price on the home. You can always opt to pay for them in cash or persuade your lender to factor them into your mortgage loan so that you can pay for them slowly with time.

During this phase, the money is usually moved to escrow and remains there until all details regarding the transaction have been confirmed as being satisfactory to all participants. After that has happened, the money is disbursed to all parties accordingly.

It is also at this point where the escrow agent works with your attorney to prepare a new deed for you. Once you obtain the title to your property, the record is filed with the public lands office.

The title deed is evidence that you are the new proud owner of the property. At this point, you are free to make arrangements to move in as you please and even change your address in relevant databases such as those in banking.

Closing Thoughts: Points To Keep In Mind

Now let's recap some things that we have talked about throughout this book, plus a few more things that you ought to keep in mind as a first-time homebuyer.

1. *Make sure that all your debt is paid*

Getting out of debt is probably one of the best decisions you can ever make before you consider buying a home.

You see, debt is burdensome. And owning a home is a pretty expensive endeavor – even more costly than renting. So, by getting out of debt before taking the plunge to buy a home, you will be doing yourself a huge favor.

You will be reducing the stress in your life, and that can only equate to more happiness. You don't want to make your life a living hell as you pursue what is supposed to be an American dream, do you?

Furthermore, you will be increasing your attractiveness to lenders. Lenders do have a bad taste for people who are drowning in debt. Such people are a huge financial risk, and lenders are forced to proceed with caution.

2. Make sure that your credit score is good

Next, you want to make sure that your credit score is good. Lenders will be using it to base their decisions. Depending on your score, your mortgage will be cheap or just a little bit more expensive. And when you are serving a life-long mortgage, even a small difference in mortgage pricing can save you a small fortune.

Even after getting out of debt, you cannot expect your credit score to adjust immediately. It will take some time, and you will also need to take some steps to make sure that it gets even better. These steps were covered in detail earlier in this book. Refer to them whenever you need to.

3. Have an emergency fund in place

You also want to have an emergency fund that is well funded.

Owning a home can attract unexpected expenses, and you want to be fully prepared when those moments arise. So, before you begin house hunting, make sure that you have three to six months' worth of expenses tucked away safely to cater for unpleasant surprises.

4. Have a written budget in place

If you want to be confident that you will afford to own a home, then it's not just enough to assume that you can.

You need to draw a budget detailing all your expenses and how your income will fit into each one of them comfortably. Once you have that down, then you will have a good idea about what home you can afford, or if you can even afford a home at all.

5. Have enough for a down payment as well as closing costs

If you are serious about buying a home, then you better make sure that you have saved enough to cover the down payment as well as closing costs. Generally, the more you can come up with, the better.

But to be on the safe side, you should aim for at least 20% of the purchase price of your home to cover for the down payment, as well as 5% to cover for closing costs. This way, you will have enough to prevent frustrating the home buying process.

6. Get clear on what house you want and research your neighborhood

Once you have your budget down and have figured how much house you can afford, you want to get clear on the details of what kind of home you want and the features it should have.

You also want to check out the neighborhood that the home will be located to make sure that it will be convenient for you and future buyers who may express interest in it. Many things affect the quality of a neighborhood, such as schools, the presence of social amenities, noise levels, waste management, traffic, and so on. Be sure to research these aspects thoroughly.

7. *Shop for the best mortgage you can get*

Would you buy a car without trying to shop around to find the best possible deal you can get? Of course not. Most people wouldn't.

The exception, of course, is if you are already loaded with money and perceive shopping for a deal to be a waste of time that could be spent in more productive activities. But if you don't, then you owe it to yourself to shop around. In the long run, you will save a fortune.

Do your research to narrow down a list of lenders you could work with and submit applications to all of them. You should receive estimates of everything from interests to closing costs, and to fees. There is no danger of hurting your credit score because multiple inquiries made within 45 days are considered as just one.

Once you have all the information you need, you can perform an apples to apples comparison and pick the best offer you can find. Having this information is advantageous because you can negotiate even better terms with the lender you choose by showing how their offer compares with other competing lenders.

8. Before house-hunting, secure a pre-approval letter

It helps to get pre-approved by your lender before you go house hunting. This means securing a letter from your lender, showing how much you are guaranteed to get in financing should you land a deal.

In a competitive market where the seller is receiving multiple offers, this letter can mean the difference between winning on a deal and losing to your opponent. So be well prepared before you head out to the battle.

9. Shop for homes that are well within your budget

There is nothing worse than overextending yourself. You could be looking at months of difficulty down the road, which can turn your life into a living nightmare.

Even in a sellers' market where people are bidding ridiculous prices just to land a deal on a home, be sure to keep your head straight and bid within your means. If you have a solid budget drawn, you will know how far you are willing to stretch your means.

10. Hire a team of professionals

Purchasing a home is a complicated transaction. Even with the extensive knowledge provided by this book, there is only so much you can ever know. You need a team of people who are competent at what they do so that your purchase doesn't end up being one giant mistake that could haunt you for decades to come.

11. Have the house thoroughly inspected

Unless you are looking to buy a fixer-upper, the home you want to buy needs to be in good condition. The only way to verify this fact is to have a professional inspector go over the house from the foundation to the roof. If mistakes are spotted, and it turns out that they are not too serious to make you abandon the deal, then you can negotiate for a lower price with the seller.

12. Avoid opening or closing existing lines of credit before closing the deal

It is absolutely essential to keep your credit score clean. Therefore, after receiving a pre-approval letter from your lender, you should avoid making mistakes that compromise your score. One such mistake involves taking on new credit. Another involves closing existing lines of credit. Both of these actions will affect your credit utilization ratio, which happens to be a significant factor in determining your score.

13. Do not change jobs while the deal is open

Another critical mistake that could make your deal fall apart is changing jobs while you are attempting to find your home. Lenders perceive job stability to be a significant factor in determining the risk of giving you their money. So avoid destroying their faith in you by keeping your current job, at least for a while, until your deal is closed.

14. Do not move around large sums of money while the deal is open

Moving around large sums of money in your bank accounts can raise a red flag to your lender, who is likely to interpret such sums as large disguised debts. If you are in business or are expecting a huge bonus from your boss, then you can write to your lender explaining your situation. Otherwise, you might cause the lender to back out of your deal for fear that you might have money problems.

15. Have a budget for moving in

After all is said and done, and you now have keys to your new home, you will need to prepare and move. This is also one endeavor that can cost you a bundle, so you want to have some money set aside for it.

You may have to decide to handle the process alone, such as by renting a truck or a moving container. In other cases, you may prefer to hire a moving company to handle the entire process for you.

Moving companies charge different amounts depending on various factors such as distance, the weight of your shipment, the cost of paying laborers, and so on. Whatever you do, try and get an estimate of how much the exercise will cost and set aside a budget for it.

The website moving.com has a moving cost calculator that can help you come up with a realistic estimate for you to budget for.

Besides the moving costs, keep in mind that you may need to spend money on:

- Redecorating
- Buying new furniture
- Buying new appliances
- Landscaping
- Installing window treatments (curtains, blinds, etc.)

- Building fees

- Utility connection fees

- Professional house cleaning

- Painting

- Restocking your groceries (yes, that's right)

- Internet and cable

- Remember that you may have to pay for temporary storage and lodging depending on your circumstances

All these things cost money, so have a budget for that. *There will always be some costs you will incur as you seek to settle down in your new home.*

Keeps these points in mind, and you will have little trouble securing your home.

Tip: It would be great if you get a home warranty to cover stuff that's not covered by home insurance to cater for the cost of unexpected repairs that could be very costly.

Conclusion

Whew! There you have it. Now you are knowledgeable on how you can go about purchasing your first home.

You have learned a great deal. You have looked at how you can evaluate your financial situation to determine whether you qualify to be a home buyer. You have also looked at what considerations you will have to keep in mind regarding the home you want to buy, as well as the financing choices at your disposal. You have seen how you can go about finding a great deal and negotiating your place in it, all while protecting yourself against unforeseen circumstances.

I believe that you now are a sufficiently informed consumer who will be a lot wiser than over 90% of other first-time homebuyers who haven't made an effort to at least know something about what they plan on doing.

Now it is up to you to go ahead and put whatever you have learned here in practice on what may end up being the largest single financial decision of your life.

Besides that, I wish to thank you for your support by purchasing this book. You have rewarded my efforts, as well as those of the team that has worked hard to put this wonderful product in your hands. It is because of people like you that we find the motivation to keep creating and bringing useful products like this to the marketplace. I wish you all the best on your quest, and may God bless you abundantly.

Please visit our website for more helpful content like this: https://easycashforhouse.com/

Like us on Facebook: https://www.facebook.com/ebraveboy

Please follow us on Instagram: http://www.instagram.com/ebraveboy/

Get Your Free Copy Of My Book

https://ebraveboy_3ee2.gr8.com/

www.ingramcontent.com/pod-product-compliance
Lightning Source LLC
Chambersburg PA
CBHW071356210526
45465CB00001B/110